Planning a Community Oral History Project

COMMUNITY ORAL HISTORY TOOLKIT

Nancy MacKay • Mary Kay Quinlan • Barbara W. Sommer

This five-volume boxed set is the definitive guide to all aspects of successfully conducting community projects that conform to best practices in the field of oral history. What are the fundamental principles that make one oral history project fly and another falter? The existing oral history methodology literature has traditionally focused on conducting academic research. In contrast, the *Toolkit* is specifically geared toward helping people develop and implement oral history projects in schools, service agencies, historical societies, community centers, churches, and other community settings. The five concise volumes, authored by leaders in the oral history field, offer down-to-earth advice on every step of the project, provide numerous examples of successful projects, and include forms that you can adapt to your specific needs. Together, these volumes are your "consultant in a box," offering the tools you need to successfully launch and complete your community oral history project.

Volume 1: *Introduction to Community Oral History*, by Mary Kay Quinlan with Nancy MacKay and Barbara W. Sommer

Volume 2: *Planning a Community Oral History Project*, by Barbara W. Sommer with Nancy MacKay and Mary Kay Quinlan

Volume 3: *Managing a Community Oral History Project*, by Barbara W. Sommer with Nancy MacKay and Mary Kay Quinlan

Volume 4: *Interviewing in Community Oral History*, by Mary Kay Quinlan with Nancy MacKay and Barbara W. Sommer

Volume 5: *After the Interview in Community Oral History*, by Nancy MacKay with Mary Kay Quinlan and Barbara W. Sommer

For additional information on this series, visit www.LCoastPress.com.

Community Oral History Toolkit

NANCY MACKAY • MARY KAY QUINLAN • BARBARA W. SOMMER

VOLUME 2

Planning a Community Oral History Project

Barbara W. Sommer
with Nancy MacKay
and Mary Kay Quinlan

Left Coast
Press Inc.

Walnut Creek, California

LEFT COAST PRESS, INC.

1630 North Main Street, #400
Walnut Creek, CA 94596

Left Coast
Press Inc.   www.LCoastPress.com

978-1-61132-244-6 Paperback
978-1-61132-690-1 eBook

Library of Congress Cataloging-in-Publication Data

MacKay, Nancy, 1945-
  Community oral history toolkit / Nancy MacKay, Mary Kay Quinlan, and Barbara W.
Sommer
    5 v. ; cm.
  Includes bibliographical references and index.
  Contents: v. 1. Introduction to community oral history / by Mary Kay Quinlan with
Nancy MacKay and Barbara W. Sommer -- v. 2. Planning a community oral history
project / by Barbara W. Sommer, with Nancy MacKay and Mary Kay Quinlan -- v.
3. Managing a community oral history project / by Barbara W. Sommer with Nancy
MacKay and Mary Kay Quinlan -- v. 4. Interviewing in community oral history / by
Mary Kay Quinlan with Nancy MacKay and Barbara W. Sommer -- v. 5. After the
interview in community oral history / by Nancy MacKay with Mary Kay Quinlan and
Barbara W. Sommer.
  ISBN 978-1-59874-408-8 (complete set - pbk. : alk. paper) -- ISBN 978-1-61132-688-8
(complete set - consumer ebook) -- ISBN 978-1-61132-241-5 (volume 1 - pbk. : alk.
paper) -- ISBN 978-1-61132-689-5 (volume 1 - consumer ebook) -- ISBN 978-1-
61132-244-6 (volume 2 - pbk. : alk. paper) -- ISBN 978-1-61132-690-1 (volume 2
- consumer ebook) -- ISBN 978-1-61132-247-7 (volume 3 - pbk. : alk. paper) -- ISBN
978-1-61132-691-8 (volume 3 - consumer ebook) -- ISBN 978-1-61132-250-7 (volume
4 - pbk. : alk. paper) -- ISBN 978-1-61132-692-5 (volume 4 - consumer ebook) -- ISBN
978-1-61132-253-8 (volume 5 - pbk. : alk. paper) -- ISBN 978-1-61132-693-2 (volume
5 - consumer ebook)
  1. Oral history--Handbooks, manuals, etc. 2. Oral history--Methodology. 3.
Interviewing--Handbooks, manuals, etc. 4. Local history--Methodology. I. Quinlan,
Mary Kay. II. Sommer, Barbara W. III. Title.
  D16.14.M22 2012
  907.2--dc23
                              2012026513

Printed in the United States of America

  ™ The paper used in this publication meets the minimum requirements of American
National Standard for Information Sciences—Permanence of Paper
for Printed Library Materials, ANSI/NISO Z39.48–1992.

Contents

Author's Preface

The five *Toolkit* volumes take you through the steps involved in collecting first-person information in an interview setting. The volumes cover how to identify people who are witnesses to or participants in an event or way of life, how to interview them, and how to document context to help users understand the full meaning of the interviews. They also provide guidelines for preserving the interview information and making it available to others. This volume, Volume 2, focuses on the planning steps to help you successfully prepare to do these tasks.

Standard definitions of planning state it is a process for developing a scheme, program, or method that is designed to accomplish a purpose or a goal. Applying this definition of planning to oral history, the purpose of planning is to propose a process or structure for doing and supporting the interviews. Planning includes determining a mission or purpose, identifying interviewees, developing a proposed budget or project value, identifying support options, reviewing and recommending recording equipment, and determining administrative needs. An oral history plan lays out the steps through which a general idea becomes a focused set of interviews.

Project planners define a project and identify what will be needed to carry it out. They lay out a blueprint, so to speak, for a project structure. Regardless of the size of a project or the number of interviewees under consideration, this blueprint provides a guide for doing oral history interviews.

My co-authors and I have many people to thank for helping develop this planning volume. First are the responders to our survey, more about which is said in the Methodology section in Chapter 1. Their names and project affiliations are listed in Appendix A; their voices are included throughout the volume. Thank you to Jesse Heinzen, Multimedia Director, Minnesota Historical Society, for thorough and careful review and comment on equipment information. Thank you to Michael J. Lansing, Associate Professor of History at Augsburg College, for his and his public history students' input, to Carol Ahlgren, co-director of the Modern Masters Oral History Project, and to Roy Chan, Project Director, Oakland Chinatown Oral History Project, for their review of the *Toolkit* and their comments. Thank you to Mitch Allen, founder of Left Coast Press, Inc. for his support of this project. And thank you to our editor, Stefania Van Dyke, our copyeditor, Louise Bell, and our designer Lisa Devenish. Their editorial and design work is greatly appreciated, both on the individual volumes and on the *Toolkit* as a set of five interrelated volumes. Finally, this *Toolkit* gave me the opportunity to work on another publication with Mary Kay Quinlan and to work with Nancy MacKay for the first time. Our many telephone calls, meetings, and emails strengthened the *Toolkit* volumes, including Volume 2, *Planning a Community Oral History Project*.

Barbara W. Sommer

Series Introduction

Every community has them. The people who remember

- what happened when the church burned to the ground on Christmas Eve—how the congregation grieved, and then set aside its grief, got to work, and celebrated in a new sanctuary the next year;

- how strangers with pickup trucks took tornado victims to the nearest hospital when a record-breaking storm devastated the community;

- what it was like to bring a neighborhood together to fight the city's plans for a freeway; or

- how children, teachers, and community members felt the first day black and white youngsters shared the same classrooms in the aftermath of all the lawsuits attempting to block school integration.

Old newspaper clippings tell part of the story. So do public records that document the storm, the cost of neighborhood redevelopment, or the text of the court's decision. But what's often missing from the record is the *human* side of the issues, events, and ideas that we call history. And if you're reading the *Community Oral History Toolkit,* there's a good chance you already are thinking like an oral historian. You understand that it's important to add to the historical record first person information that can flesh out or reshape our understanding of past events.

Collectively, we three *Toolkit* authors have spent more than half a century working with community oral history projects, observing along the way how some succeed and others languish. You can readily find an excellent body of literature on oral history methodology, but it is designed for academic research and often does not translate well for unaffiliated community groups. So we've attempted in this five-volume *Toolkit* to identify some fundamental principles that lead to successful community oral history projects and to present practical tools and guidelines that we hope will be useful in a variety of community settings.

Defining Oral History

We define *community* broadly, using the definition found in the Oral History Association's pamphlet *Using Oral History in Community History Projects* (2010). The pamphlet defines community as any group of individuals bound together by a sense of shared identity. For the purposes of this *Toolkit*, we consider community oral history as that being undertaken by any group unaffiliated with an academic institution. Such groups could be neighborhood associations, historical societies, museums, libraries, professional associations, clubs, or any of the myriad ways people organize themselves to accomplish particular ends. Because we consider *community* in its broadest sense, we've included examples of community oral history projects that are diverse in size, topic of study, sponsoring organization, geographic location, and project goals. As you move through your own oral history project, and through the five *Toolkit* volumes, we encourage you to define your own community in the way that works best for you.

Community oral history projects differ in many ways from those originating in an academic setting. They usually

- lack institutional support for planning, managing, or funding;
- are organized around an exhibition, festival, performance, or publication;
- are driven by grant cycles and deadlines, sometimes with a specific goal determined by the funder;
- are carried out by volunteers or by a single paid staff member supervising volunteers;
- barter with local businesses or agencies for office space, technology expertise, and supplies;
- lack infrastructure, such as office space, storage, and computer equipment; and
- almost always have limited funds.

This *Toolkit* recognizes the special challenges community oral historians face and suggests ways to deal with them. It is predicated on the notion that a well-funded institutional setting is not a prerequisite to create solid oral history projects that will endure over time. What is required, however, is a fundamental understanding of oral history as a process that begins long before you ask the first interview question and ends long after you turn off the recorder.

For starters, here's how oral history is defined throughout these five volumes.

Oral history is primary source material collected in an interview setting with a witness to or a participant in an event or a way of life and is grounded in context of time and place to give it meaning. It is recorded for the purpose of preserving the information and making it available to others. The term refers to both the process and the final product.

What You'll Find in the *Community Oral History Toolkit*

The *Community Oral History Toolkit* consists of five individual volumes. Each volume covers a particular aspect of doing oral history. Although each volume stands alone, the *Toolkit* is best seen as an integrated reference set, in much the same way that any particular aspect of doing oral history is dependent on decisions made at other stages of the process. The *Toolkit* is tightly organized, with subheadings, cross references within the text, and a comprehensive index for ready reference. You'll also find various visual elements, including hot spots (concise tips), definitions, sidebars (case studies and extended discussions), checklists, and figures that illustrate, elaborate, or draw attention to specific points. While all three of us have collaborated throughout the project, we divided the writing duties for the five volumes. Barbara Sommer is the lead author of Volumes 2 and 3; Mary Kay Quinlan is the lead author of Volumes 1 and 4; and Nancy MacKay is the lead author of Volume 5 and overall project coordinator, spearheading the research phase, marshaling the final details and keeping us all on task.

Volume 1. Introduction to Community Oral History. This volume sets the stage for your oral history project. It introduces the field to newcomers, with a discussion of the historical process, the evolution of oral history as an interdisciplinary research methodology, the nature of community and the nature of memory, and the legal and ethical underpinnings of oral history. And as such, Volume 1 importantly lays the theoretical groundwork for the practical application steps spelled out in detail in the subsequent volumes. It also introduces recording technology issues and options for oral history preservation, access, and use. Last, this volume elaborates on our Best Practices for Community Oral History Projects and presents a detailed overview of the remaining *Toolkit* volumes.

BEST PRACTICES
for Community Oral History Projects

1. **Familiarize yourself with the Oral History Association's guidelines.** First developed in 1968 and revised and updated regularly since then, these guidelines are the benchmark for the practice of ethical oral history and form the foundation on which solid oral history projects are built. Becoming familiar with them will help your project get off to a strong start.

2. **Focus on oral history as a process.** Keep in mind that, using standard historical research methods, you are setting out to explore a historical question through recorded interviews, giving it context and preserving it in the public record—in addition to whatever short-term goals your project may have such as using interview excerpts to create an exhibit or celebrate an anniversary.

3. **Cast a wide net to include community.** Make sure all appropriate community members are involved in your project and have an opportunity to make a contribution. Community members know and care the most about the project at hand, and the more closely they are involved in every aspect of it, the more successful it will be.

4. **Understand the ethical and legal ramifications of oral history.** Oral historians record deeply personal stories that become available in an archive for access both in the present and the future. So oral historians have ethical and legal responsibilities to abide by copyright laws and respect interviewees' wishes while also being true to the purposes of oral history.

Volume 2. Planning a Community Oral History Project. This volume walks you through all the planning steps needed to travel from an idea to a completed collection of oral history interviews. It will help you get started on firm ground, so you don't end up mired in quicksand halfway through your project or trapped in a maze of seemingly unsolvable problems.

Volume 3. Managing a Community Oral History Project. This volume takes the planning steps and puts them into action. It provides the practical details for turning your plans into reality and establishes the basis for guiding your project through the interviews and to a successful conclusion.

Volume 4. Interviewing in Community Oral History. The interview is the anchor of an oral history project. This volume guides the interviewer through all the steps from interview preparation to the follow-up. It includes tips on

5. **Make a plan.** At the outset, define your purpose, set goals, evaluate your progress, and establish record-keeping systems so details don't get out of control.

6. **Choose appropriate technology with an eye toward present and future needs.** Technology is necessary for recording interviews, preserving them in an archive, and providing access and using them for public displays. Make wise decisions about the technology you use.

7. **Train interviewers and other project participants to assure consistent quality.** Oral history interviews differ from some other interview-based research methods in the amount of background research and preparation required. Make sure interviewers and other personnel are thoroughly trained in oral history principles, interviewing techniques, recording technology, and ethics. The *Community Oral History Toolkit* covers all these topics.

8. **Conduct interviews that will stand the test of time.** This is the heart of the oral history process, but its success depends on laying solid groundwork.

9. **Process and archive all interview materials to preserve them for future use.** Oral history interviews and related materials should be preserved, cataloged, and made available for others to use in a suitable repository, such as a library, archive, or historical society.

10. **Take pride in your contribution to the historical record.** Share with the community what you've learned, and celebrate your success.

---

selecting interviewees, training interviewers, using recording equipment, and assessing ethical issues concerning the interviewer-interviewee relationship.

Volume 5. After the Interview in Community Oral History. Community projects often falter after the interviews are completed. This volume explains the importance of processing and archiving oral histories and takes readers through all the steps required for good archiving and for concluding an oral history project. It finishes with examples of creative ways community projects have used oral histories.

Finally, sample forms, checklists, and examples from the experiences of other community projects are provided that will help guide your project planning and a selected bibliography that will lead you to additional in-depth information on the various topics covered in the *Toolkit*.

We hope you will keep these volumes close at hand as you work step by step through your oral history project. Remember that the effort you put into doing the project right will pay off in unexpected ways far into the future. Many years from now you may well remember the exact words, tone of voice, or facial expression of an interviewee in answering questions only you thought to ask. And you may take satisfaction in knowing that your effort has preserved an important story—a piece of history that gives meaning to all our lives, both now and in the future.

Nancy MacKay, Mary Kay Quinlan, and Barbara W. Sommer

Toolkit Contents

Introduction

Maybe it happens at a college reunion or at a neighborhood potluck. Or maybe the cultural center where your work has received a grant to document the center's history but no one at the center knows how. It can happen any time or any place, but most community oral history projects begin with an "aha moment" when someone realizes, "We've got a story to tell and it needs to be recorded and preserved for future generations." Planting the seed for an oral history project is the first step. Sometimes months or years pass before the idea for an oral history project is implemented. But the idea comes first. Don't let this important moment pass.

As Executive Director of Oakland Asian Cultural Center, Anne Huang mixed with the locals in Oakland's Chinatown every day. In restaurants, in businesses, in dance and cooking classes offered at the Center, Anne heard stories, casually told, of old times in Chinatown—immigration stories, stories of a family business, of learning English, and of learning new ways. She had never heard of oral history, but she knew she was in the midst of a treasure trove of stories, and not only that, of an important slice of history that could only be documented within this community. Coincidentally, a history graduate student was working at the Center and a chance conversation turned to the topic of oral history as a way of documenting recent history at the local level.

At this point the seed was planted. Anne was sold on oral history as a way of accomplishing her purpose. She learned about oral history and the Oakland Asian Cultural Center conducted a successful oral history project, capturing the stories of elders, and at the same time, the history of a community in its members' own words. The oral histories now are held in libraries to help future generations understand this important way of life.

Does this sound familiar? Often oral history projects begin as a vague sense that the collective story of a community needs to be told; or conversely, as an urgent response to a piece of history that is rapidly disappearing. Community leaders hear about oral history and decide to use it for their purpose. They have access to community networks and they know the local stories. But they often lack expertise on doing oral history.

That's where this planning volume comes in. Many communities new to oral history will conduct some interviews and be done with it. We believe there is more to preserving community stories than that and project planning can help make the difference. Through project planning, community members can design a structure that supports doing, preserving, and maintaining access to oral history interviews and interview information—protecting the stories for many generations to come.

Methodology and Volume Organization

Preparation for this volume took much time and thought. My co-authors and I wanted to cover the information most helpful to community oral historians. Our efforts combined research and hands-on interaction. We did literature searches, read and reviewed oral history publications and comments on the oral history listserv (H-Oralhist), attended the annual Oral History Association meetings, participated in planning several community oral history projects, and discussed and reviewed planning steps in community oral history workshops. All of this helped us think about planning and its importance to oral history.

In addition to our own experience, we wanted to know how other oral history practitioners approach project planning. Based on our research and community outreach, we developed a short planning survey and sent it to community oral historians across the country. On it, we identified basic oral history planning steps and asked for comments about each one.

The results of the survey were enlightening. Respondents were forthcoming with information and insights about what worked for them—and what didn't. They commented on planning teams, the role of a planning director, mission statements, interviewer training, transcribing, equipment, repositories, budgets, grants—all steps that are part of oral history planning. Throughout this volume, you will find their quotes and comments about community oral history project planning. See Appendix A for a copy of the planning survey and a list of participating oral historians.

We also developed three fictitious community oral history projects for use in the *Toolkit*. We designed them to vary in type and size to illustrate the variety of oral history options for communities. Throughout this volume, I'll discuss how each fictitious project can most effectively use community oral history planning.

This volume is organized around the list of oral history planning steps presented in the checklist at the end of this chapter. Each step represents a piece of an oral history project structure. They are listed in a suggested order for making decisions as you move through the planning phase of your project. For example, you will find familiarizing yourselves with legal standards and ethical guidelines toward the top of the list, because this information is central to oral history methodology and provides a foundation for many of the remaining steps. You also will find a step about developing the project focus before the naming step, because giving a project a name usually follows defining what a set of interviews will be about.

This decision-making order probably will not be the order in which you actually use the planning steps, however. For example, as a planning and management guide (see also **Volume 3,** ***Managing a Community Oral History Project*),** we are introducing a Project Design Statement. On this form, you'll see the project name comes first because a name, once decided on, becomes a standard identifier and, from then on, is always listed first. Continuing the example, practical application of legal standards and ethical guidelines takes place on a continuing basis, so you may find reference to this information in several places on the form, not just at the beginning. You may also find that, even though your community oral history idea may have been inspired by stories from possible interviewees, the actual planning step identifying the list of interviewees comes after you define the focus and scope, because this order for decision making reflects the reality of your project planning. As you work through the planning steps for your project, I recommend you follow the order suggested in this chapter, even though practicalities may well dictate a different order for carrying them out, once your decisions are made and you move to the project management stage.

Oral History

Everyone loves a story, and communities are full of them. How could a community resist getting together to talk about the year the river crested and nearly destroyed the neighborhood, or the time a general strike in the city had unexpected consequences in the neighborhood, or even about the Hungarian stew made each year by an elderly neighbor with a unique accent and unknown past? Stories naturally lead to the idea of interviews, and the idea of interviews leads to the idea of oral history. But there is a difference between telling stories and producing oral histories.

 Oral history is more than storytelling.

What exactly is oral history? There are many definitions; the one given in the Series Introduction focuses on process. It points out that an interviewee (sometimes called a narrator)—the person whose stories and memories are recorded in an oral history interview—is someone who understands and can communicate information about their context and meaning, and that interview information should be preserved and made accessible for future users. This definition, with its reminder that oral histories are primary source documents, guides our planning discussion.

Oral History Quotes

What does oral history look or sound like? Before we go any further, let's briefly look at excerpts from two community oral history projects. You'll have to imagine hearing the actual voices, but the words speak volumes about the community each represents. Both are from planned projects and both continue to be actively used. They represent the types and variety of information that, through oral history, communities can document about themselves.

The Cushman Motor Works Oral History Project was conducted by plant employees in honor of the company's centennial. Cushman Motor Works was founded to manufacture motors and engines. It now is a manufacturer of industrial vehicles and custom vehicles. This story of the foundry described the place where large quantities of metal were melted and poured by hand into molds. Mary Kay Quinlan and I provided oral history project planning guidance and interviewer training. The publication cited in the first Note at the end of this volume was a planned project product.

The Commission of Deaf, DeafBlind and Hard of Hearing Minnesotans Oral-Visual History Project interviews were done either in spoken English or in American Sign Language (ASL) and recorded in broadcast-quality

The Cushman Motor Works Oral History Project

"The foundry was quite an interesting place. ... It was real tough work. I will never forget the smell. They used to use molasses mixed with core sand to make the cores for the molds. Of course, when they poured the hot metal in, you could smell molasses. I can always remember the foundry area smelled like that. You could tell when they were pouring from the smell. ... But I remember it was a dirty, hot place to work."[1]

Interview with Dick Pearce, Nebraska State Historical Society, Lincoln, NE, 2001.

The Commission of Deaf, DeafBlind and Hard of Hearing Minnesotans Oral-Visual History Project

LB: "I finally said I just wanted to go to the Legislature and testify. ... I was really excited to testify on behalf of DBSM [DeafBlind Services of Minnesota]. ... There I was at the committee hearing. I was called to testify. I got right up there. I said 'hello' to each one of the legislators and I said, 'I am here to tell you the truth.' Well, that got their attention. I explained everything – how DeafBlind people need SSP [Support Service Provider] services, just how critical it is to have SSPs for us to be able to interact fully and safely in the community. It was important for going to the store, in part to protect us from other people who maybe wanted to take advantage of us and any number of things. I can't remember all I said. But when I was done, I thanked them all and sat back. ... We got big money out of that one. Oh, man, I can't even remember how much it was."[2]

Interview with Lynette Boyer. Teika Pakalns, Interviewer. Alan Kenney, Tactile Interpreter. Patty Gordon and Cori Giles, Sign Language Interpreters. Lynette Boyer (voiced by Patty Gordon): LB. Teika Pakalns (voiced by Evonne Bilotta-Burke): TP. June 8, 2011. Commission of Deaf, DeafBlind and Hard of Hearing Minnesotans, St. Paul, MN.

video format. A master copy of each interview was maintained as recorded. For accessibility purposes, a copy of each ASL interview was translated into spoken English by certified interpreters and voiceovers were added. All interviews were also transcribed and closed captioned. This project, called an oral-visual history project to indicate its roots in the oral history process with use of a visual language as the primary interview language, provides information about deaf, deafblind, and hard of hearing people and their community activism in Minnesota. The project was supported in part with funds generated for environmental and legacy projects by a clean water, land, and legacy tax in Minnesota. All materials are available through the Commission of Deaf, DeafBlind, and Hard of Hearing Minnesotans, St. Paul, MN, http://www.mncdhh.org/heritage/.

Documenting Community History Through Oral History

The *Toolkit* emphasizes the idea of taking a community's stories—the information that shapes a community's identity—and formulating them into *community oral history projects*. What does this mean?

By **community**, we mean any group of individuals bound together by a shared identity.

Community oral history is oral history that is not aligned with academic instruction. As you'll see when we work through the planning process, community oral history draws on members of a community to plan and organize interviews as well as provide the people whose information—the memories—will be recorded.

Oral historians work to well-defined standards. We have defined these standards for community oral history projects in our ten Best Practices for Community Oral History Projects. The Series Introduction in each *Toolkit* volume contains a complete set of these practices. To help project planners apply the Best Practices for Community Oral History Projects, each chapter begins with the particular practices it most directly references. The three Best Practices for this chapter introduce community oral history project planning, focusing on the importance of the oral history process and on using a plan to get organized.

> *Best Practice No. 1:* **Familiarize yourself with the Oral History Association's guidelines.** As the description of this Best Practice states, these guidelines are the standards to which oral historians work. Read

them and keep a copy in the project files. Review them regularly as a reminder of what you're doing and why.

Best Practice No. 2: **Focus on oral history as a process.** This Best Practice encourages oral historians to put the interview into context through careful and thorough preparation. It reminds us that doing oral history interviews is a multi-step process.

Best Practice No. 5: **Make a plan.** This Best Practice emphasizes the importance of developing a plan to guide the interviewing process.

Best Practices No. 2 and No. 5 make reference to the *oral history process* and an *oral history plan.* Let's take a closer look at what each of these means. *Oral history process* reminds us there is more to doing an interview than finding someone to talk to and turning on a recorder. It involves recognizing and respecting the role of the planning steps in building an oral history structure for the interviews. An *oral history plan* is a detailed proposal on how to organize the process to achieve a specific result—a set of *community oral history interviews.*

Most interviews are recorded as part of an oral history project. *Community oral history projects* are an interrelated set of interviews about an event or way of life in a community. Projects have a common design and interview focus. Large or small, they are based in the community whose history they help document.[3] Each project is important for the information it contains and the gift of history it gives back to the community.

Sample (fictitious) community oral history projects

Just as communities vary in size and complexity, so also do community oral history projects. Some community oral history projects may result in a couple of interviews. Others may be large and ongoing, recording many interviews over a period of years. Regardless of size and complexity, however, all can benefit from project planning. To illustrate this point, we use three fictitious community oral history projects as examples. Look for these fictitious projects throughout this and subsequent volumes of the *Toolkit*; in this volume they help show how careful consideration of planning steps can benefit many types of projects.

- *Project One—Volunteer:* a small neighborhood oral history project without a budget
- *Project Two—City:* a grant-funded project done in partnership with a city
- *Project Three—Historical Society:* a pilot project used by a historical society to launch an ongoing oral history program

Project One—Volunteer is small and relatively informal involving just a couple of interviews. It will take less than a year to complete, including planning time. The people involved want to know how to choose interviewees and develop questions. Even though the project is small, identifying a focus, scope, and project design will help guide question development, determine how many interviews the project team can effectively expect to do, and make sure legal standards are met.

Project Two—City has grant funding, which gives it support, stability, access to interviewees, and possibly a high profile. But this also can be an indication of outside influence on its timeline and goals. This situation, which could have an impact on interviewee choice and interview content, is one that project planners will want to identify and discuss in a plan.

Project Three—Historical Society is the first phase of a proposed ongoing program. Its ties to the historical society give it credibility in the community, helping the team identify supporters and future interviewees. Its proposed ongoing status can give it a sense of stability, but this perception could be deceiving if it masks a lack of internal goals, focus, and scope. Even though the program is ongoing, the planners still need to set internal project guidelines.

Watch for these sample projects throughout this *Toolkit* volume. Suggestions about how each project can use planning steps to develop a project plan are incorporated into each chapter.

Why Plan?

A plan, put in place before beginning interviews, is an essential tool for success. Think again about the stories that led to a community oral history discussion. A plan helps bridge the gap between recording often-told community stories and building a lasting gift to the community—primary source documents recorded in the form of oral histories.

Anyone who has led workshops teaching community oral history probably has heard requests for the type of information covered by a planning process. The requests come from attendees who want to know how to get started, who to interview, what kind of equipment to use, and what interview questions to ask. The nearby checklist of frequently asked questions (FAQs) about community oral history summarizes the questions most often raised. All, regardless of why they are asked, reflect a search for the type of organization and structure found in a community oral history project plan.

You don't need to try and answer these questions here. I will provide the answers in the following chapters. Watch for the information and then look for the FAQ Recap in the last chapter.

COMMUNITY ORAL HISTORY PROJECT FAQS

✓ How long does it take to do oral history interviews?

✓ How many people from the community should we involve?

✓ How about our community leaders? What is the best way to involve them?

✓ We want to do oral histories about our community, but everybody has a different idea about what this means. What should we do?

✓ How many people should we interview and who should they be?

✓ How do we figure out what questions to ask during an interview?

✓ Why do we need a Legal Release Agreement, especially if we're only doing a small number of interviews?

✓ What kind of equipment should we use? What about using our home video cameras to record our interviews?

✓ Do we need a budget?

✓ What should we do with the interviews after we've recorded them?

✓ We don't want our interviews to just sit on a shelf somewhere. How can we encourage people to use them?

✓ What do we have to do, so we can use the interviews in our upcoming community celebration?

 Most community oral history plans are developed in project format.

These are not easy questions to answer: they take time and thought. All are central to understanding the oral history process, and the answers are important parts of a community oral history plan. Answers can be anticipated and organized into a plan before beginning community oral history interviews, or they can be dealt with, with varying degrees of difficulty or success, as interviewers are doing the interviews. Speaking from experience,

> "We had a steering [planning] committee that met weekly for over a year before implementation [doing the interviews]."
>
> *Worcester (MA) Women's History Project, Oral History Initiative, Lisa Krissoff Boehm, Project Consultant*

my coauthors and I strongly recommend you develop a plan before your team starts doing interviews. Trying to do planning and interviewing at the same time—that is, pulling together answers to these FAQs while focusing on oral history interviews—can be a time and energy drain, especially for groups new to oral history. Planning provides the opportunity to develop a strong, focused project design.

Community Oral History Planning Steps

As with anything of lasting quality, planning takes time and energy, thought and preparation. When completed, a plan identifies the structure for recording a set of oral history interviews in a community.

The steps in the nearby checklist define the oral history planning process. In addition to those related specifically to interview content, they cover all levels of interview and project development. Based on methodology, they define the full structure within which oral history interviewing is done.

The steps are listed in a specific order—the probable sequence of your decision-making process. As you make your decisions based on the planning steps in this volume, understand you are developing the building blocks of a community oral history project. Once developed, these building blocks will form a recognized order and become your community oral history project structure.

COMMUNITY ORAL HISTORY PLANNING STEPS

✓ Form a project planning team and choose a planning director

✓ Identify community supporters and resource people

✓ Become familiar with oral history ethical guidelines and legal standards

✓ Define project goals, focus, scope, and write a mission statement

✓ Name the project

✓ Begin a list of project interviewees

✓ Identify suggested team member options and work space needs

✓ Make repository arrangements

✓ Develop forms and record-keeping procedures

✓ Determine equipment options

✓ Develop a project budget and identify possible funding sources

✓ Recommend after-the-interview options

✓ Assemble project plan and share it with supporters

Depending on a community's needs, some of these steps, such as identifying space needs, may be optional. Others, such as defining project focus and scope and dealing with legal standards, should be part of all community oral history plans. I'll discuss each of these steps in detail in the following chapters. Your task is to determine what will work for your plan and your community.

> "Utilizing the [planning steps] checklist provided to guide oral history project [planning], I can report our committee has accomplished [lists specific items]. We hope to begin conducting interviews as soon as possible. While the background work we've done has taken some time, it was critical to establish a solid foundation for [our] project; having the components in place establishes the credibility of the project and will help [us] qualify for grants to fund the project in the future."
>
> *Carol Ahlgren, "Modern Masters Update" in* With Respect to Architecture, *the newsletter of the Minnesota Chapter of the Society of Architectural Historians, May 2012:5.*

 Project planners propose a structure for doing oral history interviews about the past.

"The time and effort that went into planning—forming a committee, hashing out details, developing protocols, establishing a framework—allowed the project to expand in ways that couldn't be foreseen: incorporating additional voices and volunteers, obtaining grants, developing publicity and programs, etc."

Cyns Nelson/Susan Becker, From Secrecy to Accessibility: The Rocky Flats (CO) Nuclear Weapons Plant Oral Histories

"We met on a fairly regular basis to keep us all on track with so many different dimensions to this project. We had an open dialogue by email, phone and in-person with each staff person, volunteer and intern."

"Your Story and Mine: A Community of Hope," Michigan Historical Museum, Martha Aladjem Bloomfield, Project Director

CHAPTER 2

Getting Started

BEST PRACTICE NO. 2

Focus on oral history as a process.

BEST PRACTICE NO. 3

Cast a wide net to include community.

BEST PRACTICE NO. 4

Understand the ethical and legal ramifications of oral history.

BEST PRACTICE NO. 5

Make a plan.

The seed has been planted. Now let's discuss how to begin community oral history project planning. In this chapter, I'll cover the planning first steps, discuss how to form a planning team, and cover legal and ethical planning steps. As we go over these steps, I'll recommend ways to use them in a community oral history project plan.

The First Steps

Community oral history projects often begin when someone has an idea about recording some interviews. Determining what it will take to do a project is where planning comes in. Wherever and however the idea begins, it takes one person to step up and begin the discussions for it to become a project.

The idea of recording stories from the past often attracts people with an interest in hearing and sharing them. If you have an idea or story in mind, whether it is broad or focused, you should begin by getting a group together, formal or informal, to discuss it. Members of this group could transition into a project planning team and, after the planning, into a project management and interviewing team, so try to include people able to give the time, energy, and interest needed for a possible project.

After you have identified a group of community members, call a meeting to describe and discuss the idea. Think carefully about what to cover in these discussions: they help lay the groundwork for answering community oral history project FAQs. Structure the discussion by asking basic content and organizational questions and keeping track of the answers.

EXAMPLES OF GUIDING QUESTIONS

Describe the proposed project idea, and then ask:

✓ What information do we want to we collect?

✓ Why do we want to collect this information? (List all reasons, such as not losing the history of our area, celebrating an event or a particular time period.)

✓ Why do we want to use oral history to document this information? (List all reasons, such as developing a collection of first-person interviews, collecting stories for a program or publication.)

✓ Who are our potential interviewees and why would we want to interview them?

✓ What should happen to our oral histories?

✓ What are our possible project products—public programs, publication, exhibit, documentary?

Take your time and discuss the questions in detail. There are no right or wrong answers, but you should reach consensus before moving forward. These conversations will help you begin to define basic project goals, focus, and scope and to bring everyone to the same page when thinking about a possible oral history project.

Once you have completed this discussion and come to an agreement, move to a set of follow-up questions. Building on the first set, these questions further define project ideas.

EXAMPLES OF FOLLOW-UP QUESTIONS

✓ Who in our community could help us with a project like this?

✓ What anticipated costs could we have and what are possible ways to cover them?

✓ How do we think people in our community will respond to a project like this?

✓ Who will take care of the interviews and provide access to them after we've recorded them?

Review of questions like these usually takes several meetings. Again, take your time as you go through them. You are beginning to develop an outline for the design of your community oral history project.

Project Planning Team

Mention the words oral history and you will probably find many people interested in becoming involved in a project. All are possible participants, but from the beginning think about organizing three to five interested community members into a project planning team. The project planning team can, and often does, call on others in the community to help with various parts of the plan, but it's the team's responsibility to use answers to the guiding planning questions as the basis for project planning.

Throughout this volume, you will see references to both planning decisions and planning recommendations. Use your planning team to make *decisions* about the project content, name, and mission statement, and the suggested interviewee list. These are critical decisions that, once made, guide the rest of project development. Use the team also to make *recommendations* about such things as funding options, equipment options, repository options, personnel and space options, and budget options. Recommendations usually result in decisions but leave openings for management team input and involvement. I will discuss this further in **Volume 3**, *Managing a Community Oral History Project.*

 A three-to-five person project planning team develops an idea into an oral history project.

Suggested Planning Team Members

For the planning team, look for people who:

- are from the community,
- have an interest in the oral history project idea,
- can make a time commitment to see a planning process through, and
- have access to resources and knowledge that can help the planning process.

Seek out people who want to roll up their sleeves and get to work. Planning team members eventually may serve as project director, managers, and interviewers—and some may be asked to be interviewees—but, at this point, their focus should be on project planning.

 Community oral history project planning can take six months to a year.

Planning Director

The next step is to select a project planning director—the planning team's point position. A planning director agrees to take responsibility for keeping the planning team organized and moving ahead. Willingness on the part of the planning director to see the planning project through is important. A director's ability to stay with the project, if at all possible, provides continuity and stability. This person may be a member of the project planning team or someone from a sponsoring institution who is asked to step into the leadership position. Choose whichever option works best for your community.

Some projects hire a consultant either to fill the planning director position or to work closely with a director. It's not necessary to hire a consultant, but if the project planning team decides to do so, look for someone with background, experience, and knowledge related to oral history and the history of the community.

Community Supporters

Initial project planning meetings may attract many people who have an interest in oral history. Even though they won't all end up on a project planning team, don't lose sight of them or their interest in the project. Some may

Figure 2.1. A planning team discusses ideas for the Ebb and Flow Oral History Program, a series of projects that explored the heritage of local rivers, County of Suffolk, England. Image © 2007 Theo Clarke

have access to information that can support the planning process. Others may know community history or potential project supporters. And when the planning team begins to make a list of prospective interviewees, some of these supporters may be at the top of that list.

 Look to the community for supporters.

The time to start identifying community supporters is when you begin to plan. Oral history projects benefit from access to many people and many resources, but the central one for community based projects is the community. As our Best Practices for Community Oral History Projects advise, you need to attract a wide variety of supporters. Let community members know what is going on. Tell them what oral history is and why you are interested in using it to document community history. Ask for advice from people who attended the discussion meetings. Visit community leaders and discuss the idea. Request feedback and support, and ask about others who may be willing to provide support. Most important, reach out for community support and let everyone know the proposed oral history project is by, for, and about the history of the community.

 A community oral history project is by, for, and about the history of the community.

Sometimes planning team members recommend asking supporters to sit on an advisory committee or board. This arrangement probably works better for larger projects, such as our fictitious grant-funded city project (*Project Two—City*), than for smaller projects, such as our fictitious all volunteer project (*Project One—Volunteer*). An ongoing project such as our fictitious historical society project (*Project Three—Historical Society*) may find organizing an advisory board is a good way of maintaining a liaison with the community. The decision will depend on project needs and project interaction with community supporters. If the planning team recommends organizing a more formal committee or advisory board, state this in the plan and describe why the team is making the recommendation. Remember, such groups do not need to meet regularly but the members should be available to help with the project.

Regardless of what is recommended, the names of community supporters involved in your project should be included in the plan, using a supporter database. Begin early to keep track of everyone who is helping with the project plan. Include contact information and each person's relationship to the planning process. Use the list to thank people who have helped with project plans at meetings, in publicity, in emails and telephone calls, and just in general. And make sure, when you list the names, you spell them correctly.

Community Resource People

In addition to supporters, look for community resource people who can help provide information for a project plan. These are local historians and archivists/librarians knowledgeable about community history and equipment specialists, oral history practitioners, and transcribers who can provide detailed input about various planning steps.

Identify community resource people as early in project planning as you can. Let them know about the project. Explain the steps and the purpose of the plan. Discuss the possibility that, after project planning, they may be asked to continue their involvement by helping with interview preparation. And, as with supporters, include their names and contact information in a database and in the project plan.

Ethical Guidelines

Oral history is a people-to-people practice. In it, individuals, many of whom do not habitually speak into a microphone, are asked to record their knowledge and memories. They may be asked to do this with someone they don't know or with someone they know very well. Oral historians have an ethical responsibility

Community Oral History Resources

- Historians, museum curators, historical society reference personnel, and archivists/librarians can help you find background content information to focus the project and ground the interviews.

- Oral history practitioners can provide an understanding of oral history methodology and offer specialized interviewer training.

- Equipment specialists can help guide recording equipment decisions and train interviewers on using various pieces of equipment.

- Transcribers have special skills for translating the spoken word into verbatim, searchable documents.

to those who share their memories. See **Volume 1, *Introduction to Community Oral History***, for a discussion of what this means. Our Best Practices for Community Oral History summarize this information in ten basic points. Use the full discussion of these responsibilities and the best practices as ethical guides when making project planning recommendations and decisions.

For further guidance, turn to the set of guidelines developed by the Oral History Association (OHA), the professional association for oral history practitioners. These guidelines, the Oral History Association's *General Principles for Oral History* and *Best Practices for Oral History*, are on the OHA website (http://www.oralhistory.org/do-oral-history/principles-and-practices/). Throughout the planning process, keep copies of the OHA guidelines with your project planning materials. Refer to them as reminders of ethical oral history standards and include a sentence in the project plan about the planning team's commitment to maintaining oral history ethical standards throughout the duration of the project.[4]

Legal Standards

Familiarizing team members with oral history legal standards also is an important planning step. Oral history methodology recognizes interviewees and interviewers as joint authors of recorded interviews. Oral historians use *Legal Release Agreements* (often called donor forms or deeds of gift) to transfer rights to recorded interview information from interviewees and interviewers to a specified entity or third party that will preserve the interviews and make them accessible. Legal Release Agreements convey the message that interview participants are not just giving consent for use of their interview information but are recognizing an oral history interview as a copyrightable document. It is the project planning team's responsibility to become informed about oral history legal standards and to include recommended Legal Release Agreement language and a suggested form in the project plan.

Ballentine's Law Dictionary defines **copyright** as "the exclusive privilege...of an author or proprietor to print or otherwise multiply, publish, and vend copies of his literary, artistic, or intellectual productions, and to license their production and sale by others...."[5]

Oral historian John Neuenschwander covers legal issues in his book entitled *A Guide to Oral History and the Law* and in an earlier pamphlet published by the Oral History Association entitled *Oral History and the Law.* Both publications provide legal information in layman's language and both suggest policies and procedures for oral history practitioners. They are widely available and are good resources for community oral history planning directors and teams. I'll cover legal guidelines for project planners here and related management issues in **Volume 3,** *Managing a Community Oral History Project.*[6]

LEGAL STANDARDS FOR ORAL HISTORY PROJECT PLANNERS

✓ Oral history interviews are covered by copyright law.

✓ Copyright ownership begins the moment the interviewee stops speaking.

✓ Oral history interviews are recognized as as joint works.

✓ Legal Release Agreements are needed.

Let's review each item on the checklist.

Oral history interviews are covered by copyright law.

In the United States, copyright is governed by the Copyright Act of 1976 and the Digital Millennium Act of 1998. Through this law, oral history recordings are recognized as nonfiction works representing unique expressions of information fixed in a tangible medium. Copyright recognition or protection can extend as long as seventy years after the death of the last surviving author. It is rarely, if ever, filed for oral history interviews and does not need to be filed for oral histories to be copyrighted.

Copyright covers the following five points.

- reproduction
- creation of derivative works
- distribution
- public performance
- display

These five rights go into effect the moment the interview is completed and govern everything from reproduction for researcher use to using interview information in literary, musical, dramatic, and choreographic materials, including museum exhibits.

Copyright ownership begins the moment the interviewee stops speaking.

In his book, *A Guide to Oral History and the Law* (2009), John Neuenschwander described copyright ownership beginning "at the moment of creation." For oral historians, this means copyright protection begins for an interviewee, as the creator of the interview, when he or she stops talking into the recorder; it is at that point that an oral history interview becomes an original work "of authorship fixed in any tangible medium of expression" and, thus, subject to copyright law.[7]

Oral history interviews are recognized as joint works.

Copyright law does not formally recognize interviewers as co-creators of interviews, but it does recognize works that may have more than one author if the contributions by each person are "inseparable or interdependent." Oral histories appear to fall into this joint works category because contributions of interviewers and interviewees are interrelated. Both contribute to the unique final document, thus extending probable copyright protection to an interviewer. As a joint work, interviewer copyright protection applies not just to the questions asked but to the entire interview as an undivided interest.

Legal Release Agreements are needed.

The need for Legal Release Agreements is basic to the work of oral historians. It is grounded in U.S. copyright law, which treats an oral history recording as a published document and assigns ownership of its spoken words, the intellectual property, as a joint work to the interviewee and the interviewer. The agreement recognizes interview copyright and clarifies the responsibilities of everyone involved in the interview. It meets copyright law by transferring copyright in writing with a signature from the owners.[8]

Legal Release Agreements

Oral historians use *Legal Release Agreements* (often called donor forms or deeds of gift) to transfer rights for future use of recorded interview information from interviewees and interviewers to a specified entity that will preserve and provide access to them (see Figure 2.2). Use of a Legal Release Agreement recognizes an oral history interview as a copyrightable document. It is the project planning team's responsibility to become informed about oral history legal standards and to include recommended Legal Release Agreement language and a suggested form in the project plan.

Oral history publications and websites include many examples of Legal Release Agreements. As may be seen from a review of these forms, they need not be long or complex. Oral historian and legal expert John Neuenschwander recommends the language be simple and straightforward. As he wrote, "The best legal release agreements contain precise but not overly legalistic language, document the full meeting of the minds between the parties on all relevant issues, and provide a road map for future use and administration."[9]

A Legal Release Agreement may be written as a deed of gift or as a contract. Most oral history Legal Release Agreements are deeds of gift—voluntary transfers of ownership without payment. A deed of gift must reflect a donor's intent to give the gift (the interview), delivery of the interview, and acceptance of the interview. If a Legal Release Agreement is written as a contract, it must provide for a payment of some sort—usually a token amount.

Planning teams often ask for guidance in developing a Legal Release Agreement. A legal advisor can make sure the form fits a project's needs, is clearly a deed of gift or contract and not a hybrid, contains the necessary specific copyright language, and meets oral history standards. If the planning team decides to use a legal advisor, discuss basic oral history legal standards and Legal Release Agreement components with this project resource person.

COMPONENTS OF A BASIC LEGAL RELEASE AGREEMENT

✓ interviewee's name

✓ project name

✓ name of project repository or entity that will accept and hold rights to the interview

✓ a statement indicating the interviewee is transferring "legal title and all literary property rights to the interview, including copyright" to the designated repository or entity

✓ a place for signatures of the interviewer and interviewee[10]

"Sample documents are very helpful, especially for consent forms [Legal Release Agreements]. We gathered such forms from a variety of sources. ... We studied a variety of forms that I had used in past projects and found in various books, adapting the form for our needs."

Oakland (CA) Chinatown Oral History Project, Angela Zusman, Project Manager

"Developing the legal forms was most time consuming. We had help from the City Librarian, our humanities consultant and a lawyer friend who reviewed it pro bono."

The Azusa (CA) Heritage Project, Luisa Miranda, Project Director

A sample Legal Release Agreement is shown on the following page; it also is included with our set of *Toolkit* forms in **Volume 1,** *Introduction to Community Oral History.*

Starting at the top, let's review this form. It begins with the project name and mission statement. Below that is an acknowledgement of interviewee participation in the project followed by a line for the full name of an interviewee (as listed in public records). The name of a designated repository or entity accepting rights to the interview identifies where it will be preserved and made accessible on an ongoing basis. If a project repository or long-term preservation and access plan is not confirmed when interviews begin, include a temporary location agreed on by project planning team members here.

The line on the Legal Release Agreement conveying copyright transfers rights to the interview, while, as the last line in that paragraph states, allowing the interviewee rights for ongoing use as well. Legal Release Agreements may include places for interviewer and interviewee signatures on one form, as shown here, or the planning team may recommend separate agreements for interviewers and interviewees.

After an interview, an interviewee may ask to control access to it. This is rare, but if it happens, use a Legal Release Agreement (Restrictions) (see Figure 2.3). The form is similar to the Legal Release Agreement, but it includes a provision for limiting access to an interview for a specific period of time.

Legal Release Agreements will be some of your most important project documents. Most repositories will not take oral history interviews without a signed Legal Release Agreement for each interview.

LEGAL RELEASE AGREEMENT

The mission of the _____(oral history project) is to document

the history of _____. The major part of this effort is the collection

of oral history interviews with knowledgeable individuals.

Thank you for participating in our project. Please read and sign this gift agreement so your

interview will be available for future use. Before doing so, you should read it carefully and ask any

questions you may have regarding terms and conditions.

AGREEMENT

I, _____ , interviewee, donate and convey my oral history

interview dated _____ to the _____

(oral history project/repository name). In making this gift I understand that I am conveying all right,

title, and interest in copyright to the oral history project/repository. I also grant the oral history

project/repository the right to use my name and likeness in promotional materials for outreach

and educational materials. In return, the oral history project/repository grants me a non-exclusive

license to use my interview through my lifetime.

I further understand that I will have the opportunity to review and approve my interview before it is

placed in the repository and made available to the public. Once I have approved it, the oral

history project/repository will make my interview available for research without restriction. Future

uses may include quotation in printed materials or audio/video excerpts in any media, and

availability on the Internet.

INTERVIEWEE	INTERVIEWER
Name (print) _____	Name (print) _____
Signature _____	Signature _____
Date _____	Date _____

Figure 2.2. Legal Release Agreement

LEGAL RELEASE AGREEMENT (RESTRICTIONS)

The mission of the _____(oral history project) is to document

the history of _____. The major part of this effort is the collection

of oral history interviews with knowledgeable individuals.

Thank you for participating in our project. Please read and sign this gift agreement so your

interview will be available for future use. Before doing so, you should read it carefully and ask any

questions you may have regarding terms and conditions.

AGREEMENT

I, _____ , interviewee, donate and convey my oral history

interview dated, _____ to the _____

(oral history project/repository name). In making this gift I understand that I am conveying all right,

title, and interest in copyright to the oral history project/repository. I also grant the oral history

project/repository the right to use my name and likeness in promotional materials for outreach

and educational materials. In return, the oral history project/repository grants me a non-exclusive

license to use my interview throughout my lifetime.

I understand that I will have the opportunity to review and approve my interview before it is placed

in the repository. My gift and the associated rights are subject to the following restrictions:

_____ May not be made available on the Internet

_____ Public access may not be available until (date) _____ _____

_____ Other (specify) _____

INTERVIEWEE	INTERVIEWER
Name (print) _____	Name (print) _____
Signature _____	Signature _____
Date _____	Date _____

Figure 2.3. Legal Release Agreement (Restrictions)

CHAPTER 3

Project Design

BEST PRACTICE NO. 2

Focus on oral history as a process.

BEST PRACTICE NO. 5

Make a plan.

Some years ago, the India Association of Minnesota began working with the Minnesota Historical Society to develop an oral history project about the immigrant experience. The two-part project design planned through this collaboration included two years of interviews with fifteen interviewees—all immigrants from India—followed by two years of interviews with fifteen members of first-generation Indian Americans, including many children of the first-round interviewees. Project goals focused on adding information about the immigrant experience in a new culture to the historical record and documenting differences between first and second generation immigrant families. The two parts of this project, done over a span of five years, helped document information about immigration and acculturation from several, sometimes divergent, points of view. The project has since expanded to include additional interviewees, broadening the range of the discussion.

A community oral history project starts with an idea just like this. There is a gap in the historical record, perhaps, or you hear community stories you don't want to lose. In this chapter we'll discuss how to take an idea and focus it, which should help project planners answer more community oral history FAQs, especially those about who to interview and what questions to ask.

Oral history practitioners focus on the past, work in the present, and plan for the future.

In this chapter, I'll introduce the Project Design Statement and cover the following project planning steps: defining the project goals, focus, scope, and writing a mission statement; naming the project; and beginning a list of project interviewees.

Project Design Statement

As soon as you start project planning, develop a system to keep track of your decisions. This will keep your project planning organized and will be a useful resource for future users of your interview information. Many project planning teams, in addition to keeping notes about decisions, develop forms or other organizational aids to track project development and design. These forms need not be fancy; the more straightforward they are, the easier they are to work with. The Project Design Statement is an example of a form developed for this purpose.

As you make your decisions or recommendations for each of the planning steps listed in Chapter One of this volume, enter the information on the Project Design Statement. Line items on the form are keyed to the planning steps; they should provide adequate space to state your decision and add details as needed. Note, however, as you use this form that the information is organized in suggested use order rather than suggested decision-making order. The project name is at the top of the form even though it is not the first decision you will make. The mission statement is listed at the top of the form because of its importance in defining project design, even though, because of its dependence on planning decisions that come before it, it is further down the decision-making list. Fill in the form as you complete your project planning steps; when you have completed the steps, you should have completed the form as well. Listing an item on the form indicates its acceptance by the project planning team as a planning component. The Project Design Statement, when completed, becomes an anchor for your project (see Figure 3.1).

 Develop a process early on for keeping track of planning decisions.

PROJECT DESIGN STATEMENT	
GENERAL	
PROJECT NAME Insert project name	
SPONSORING INSTITUTION List if applicable	
PRIMARY GOAL List 1-3 major goals	
MISSION STATEMENT Insert project mission statement	
ADMINISTRATIVE REQUIREMENTS List project team member roles	
PROJECT CONTENT	
HISTORICAL FOCUS Describe project focus; be specific	
SCOPE Summarize project scope, including size and duration	
TOPICS List project topics; use bullet points if needed	
SOURCES FOR BACKGROUND RESEARCH Summarize sources and locations; refer to project bibliography	
PROJECT MANAGEMENT	
DURATION Describe specific project duration; if part of an ongoing program, state this	
NUMBER OF INTERVIEWEES State number of interviewees and document decision; use bullet points as needed	
RECORDING PLAN Describe recorders (audio, video, or both) and summarize use plan	
PHYSICAL SPACE NEEDS Summarize interviewing and project work space needs	
EXPENSES Summarize project expenses (known or projected) by type; refer to project budget for detailed information	
RESOURCES Summarize project resources by type (for example: volunteer, donation/gift, grant); refer to project budget for detailed information	
INTERVIEWEE RECRUITMENT Summarize interviewee recruitment process; refer to Interviewee Recommendation Form	
REPOSITORY PLAN Summarize repository plan and include names and contact information for repository personnel; note use of Letter of Agreement for Repository	
ONLINE ACCESS FOR INTERVIEWS Summarize online access plan; include websites and URLs	
Submitted by Project Director	**Date**
Revised by Use if project revisions are needed	**Date**

Figure 3.1. Annotated Project Design Statement

Some of the items on the Project Design Statement may seem too detailed for community oral history projects, especially for smaller ones like our fictitious all-volunteer project (*Project One—Volunteer*). If this is the case for your project, adapt the form to your needs. But this is where thinking like an oral historian comes in. When project planners take the time to define the project goals, focus, and scope and to write a mission statement, it's easier to recommend who to interview and what to ask—basic oral history project decisions—regardless of the size of the project. The interview content section of the form gives project planners a place to spell out these decisions. See **Volume 3, *Managing a Community Oral History Project*** for examples of completed Project Design Statement forms for our fictitious projects.

Begin using a form like this as soon as you start planning a project—with the understanding you won't be able to fill everything in right away. Keep the form handy throughout the planning process and fill in information as you make your decisions and define your plans. Include a completed copy of the form in a project plan.

Project Goals, Historical Focus, and Scope

This section covers the basics of project design. The mission statement, which spells out the goals, focus, and scope, and project name, is covered at the end of the section.

Goals

A goal is a point or achievement toward which people work. Community oral history project goals define the project design structure. Goal statements are not long or complex. Most often, they describe the use of oral history to fill gaps in a community's history or to add new voices to the record. Goals also can define planned project products such as exhibits, events, or publications.

Most projects are designed to represent all sides of issues. Some projects, however, may be organized with a more specific or narrow goal in mind. If a project has a specific goal, such as documenting farm foreclosures from the viewpoints of farmers only, the goal statement should state this because it will have a direct impact on project design.

Historical Focus

According to Laurie Mercier and Madeline Buckendorf in *Using Oral History in Community History Projects* (2007), community oral history projects seem "to have a built-in focus—the history of the community." But, as the authors point out, this is too broad a statement to be an effective project focus.[11]

Community Oral History Primary Goals
Using Fictitious Examples

- The goal of the Fairview (NY) Business Oral History Project is to use oral history to add information about mid-20ᵗʰ century businesses in the historic North Central community to the historical record.

- The goal of the University Alumni Oral History Project is to use oral history to document the mid-to-late 20ᵗʰ century history of the Association and its support of the University during this period.

- The goal of the Fairfax (KS) Oral History Project is to use oral history to document farm foreclosures following the economic downturn in the 1980s from the viewpoints of foreclosed farmers.

- The goal of the Worthington (CA) Oral History Project is to use oral history to record information about the history of the community for a centennial publication and production of a documentary.

Think back to the story or stories that planted the idea of an oral history. What are they and how many different directions could you go with them in a series of interviews? Maybe the story that caught your ear was told by a child of immigrants who grew up in the community, went to school in the community, and then started a successful business in it. The person has had many experiences and has much to offer. You could do an oral history that would document his life experiences. But you want to use the story as a springboard for documenting community history, so how do you define the focus? Do you concentrate on the community's business and economic history? Its history of education? The history of a neighborhood? The community's recent immigration history? Each of these is an example of a project *focus*—the central idea around which a project is developed.

EXAMPLES OF QUESTIONS THAT GUIDE HISTORICAL FOCUS

✓ What was the consensus in the original discussions regarding the purpose of our project, and how can it guide us?

✓ What are possible historical focus ideas? For example, do we want to document the history of businesses in our community?

✓ If so, how many businesses are there in the community? Is there a way to narrow the focus to certain kinds of businesses?

✓ What are some unique topics or events within this broader focus that are not fully documented, such as the impact of building the first shopping mall, growth of women-owned businesses, or revitalization of a historic neighborhood business center?

✓ What are the planning team's interests and priorities regarding each of these themes or events and why?

✓ Which ideas are already documented, at least partially? Is the documentation accurate and fully representative of the community? How could an oral history project make a difference?

✓ What information would a project with this focus cover? Would it provide us, for example, additional information about business and economic activity that is vital to an understanding of the history of the community?

✓ Could the information be effectively covered in five to twelve interviews? If not, how should we handle this?

✓ Who are the possible interviewees for each project? What is their availability? Are their stories already on record? What about voices not on the record?

✓ Which historical focus idea would best represent the community or most effectively add new voices to the historical record and why?

Begin developing a historical focus by reviewing the early discussions about your original oral history idea or story. Use this as a guide when you move forward. Also turn to your community resource people to help you identify information about your community that is already on the record and what may be missing. Review your options and come to a consensus.

Once your planning team has come to an agreement about a historical focus, the next step is to think about specifics. Perhaps you have decided to pick up the business history idea as a focus. A search by your community resource people, however, turned up many businesses scattered throughout various neighborhoods, each with a list of possible interviewees. There are many ways to narrow the focus. Do you want to concentrate on businesses operating during a specific time period, a specific type of business, or a businesses operating in a specific neighborhood? Or are you interested in women-owned businesses in the community?

Continue to check with your community resource people. Look further into what is already on the record. Read old newspapers and community histories. Whose voices are not heard or represented? As you discuss the questions, keep in mind that the strength of oral history is not duplicating information already on the record, but in adding new information to it. Recommend a project focus that fills in gaps in your community history or adds previously unheard voices to the record.

 Plan on using oral history to fill gaps and add new voices to your community history.

Take your time with this part of community oral history project planning. Your decisions about historical focus are some of the most important ones you'll make.

One-Sided and Multi-Sided Historical Focus

As you think about historical focus, remember that, unless a project has a specific, stated, one-sided focus, or built-in bias, project planners should make it clear that people with information on all sides of issues should be interviewed. For example, let's say a planning team for *Project Three—Historical Society*, having decided to begin an ongoing oral history program with a business history project, defined a project documenting the impact of the first major suburban shopping mall on the community. Unless specified differently, planning team members should suggest interviewing people who have information and memories about the full impact of this event. This would include one or two people from an established community business center who lost their businesses when the shopping mall came in, community members whose businesses stayed where they were and continued to operate, owners of businesses who relocated to the shopping mall, owners of new businesses in the shopping mall, elected city or community officials with perspective on changes in the business community during this period, shopping mall developers, and others in the community who were part of or witness to this event and time in the community's history. An example of a one-sided focus, on the other hand, would involve interviews only with members of the community representing one of these issues, such as people who lost businesses when the shopping center was built. Whether your project focus is fully representational or one-sided has a direct impact on design, interview content and context, and future use of the interview information. This should be clearly stated in your plan.

Historical Focus and Interview Content

One of the most frequently asked questions in community oral history workshops is "How do we figure out what questions to ask?" Interview content is the information from each interviewee, recorded as part of a community oral history project interview. We cover interview content in more detail in **Volume 3,** *Managing a Community Oral History Project* and *Volume 4, Interviewing in Community Oral History.* For planning purposes, remember that interview questions are based on and broadly defined by project goals and focus.

Within a project's focus, interview content is defined by *topics*. For example, continuing the shopping mall illustration, interview topics could begin with a discussion of when each interviewee first heard about the proposal and how it was presented to the community. Additional topics could include questions about each interviewee's response to the news, each interviewee's experiences before, during, and after the mall opened, and interviewee descriptions of its impact on businesses and on the community.

As project planners, you should identify suggested interview topics as part of the discussion on goals and focus. To do this, work with your community resource people. Look again at the information already on the record and decide what is missing about your community. Make a list of topics and include it as part of the focus discussion in the project plan.

Historical Focus and Context

Thinking about project context reminds us that events don't happen in a vacuum. As you recommend a project focus, keep *context*—the broader threads of history, such as business or economic trends in your region and state—in mind. If you decide to look at all sides of the shopping mall issue, for example, the context will be the impact of shopping mall development on communities. If you recommend the more narrow focus, the context will be the impact of shopping mall development on lost businesses. The set of information collected for each approach adds to the knowledge about economic development in the community, but each has a specific historical meaning. Include in your project plan a statement about the context of the recommended historical focus, both as a reminder to explore the broader meanings of community stories during project interviews and as an illustration of the link between the community and the surrounding area or region.

Scope

Project *scope* describes the size and length of a project. It gives a project direction and boundaries. Define scope by recommending project duration and number of interviews.

Defining scope gives a community oral history project boundaries.

"Collecting oral histories is one of CVM's principal research techniques. This is an on-going program rather than a project."

Chippewa Valley Museum (WI), Susan McLeod, Director

"Planning issues involved choosing narrators [interviewees], insuring a balance of viewpoints, deciding on big areas of interest on which to base questions, formulating a list of broad questions for each group of participants, obtaining funding to augment both volunteer work and work funded by the Maria Rogers Oral History Program, and working out transcription conventions."

Dorothy Ciarlo/Susan Becker, From Secrecy to Accessibility: The Rocky Flats (CO) Nuclear Weapons Plant Oral Histories

Scope and Duration

Oral history projects vary in the way they are organized. Some have defined end dates and others are ongoing. Planning teams need to decide whether interviewing will continue indefinitely or will be completed within a certain time frame.

Mapping out possible workflow and milestones can help determine project duration. It's fine to change along the way—and situations may come up that bring about changes—but recommending a specific duration helps answer the community oral history FAQ about how long a project will last. By putting such project boundaries in place, project planning team members help define expectations about what a project can realistically accomplish. This is as important for small projects such as the fictitious all-volunteer project (*Project One—Volunteer*) as it is for larger projects.

Additionally, project duration is as important for ongoing programs as it is for closed-ended projects. When programs are ongoing, such as our fictitious historical society project (*Project Three—Historical Society*), internal milestones take the place of duration statements and help keep an ongoing program on track and expectations realistic.

Some projects have funding cycles that dictate specific results at certain times. If this is a possibility for your project, reflect it in your plan. Include any anticipated funding requirements or deadlines as you map out projected workflow and milestones. This likely is a factor project planners would consider in our fictitious city project (*Project Two—City*).

> "The grant period…helped guide the planning process given the limited time allotted to meet goals."
>
> *The Azusa (CA) Heritage Project, Luisa Miranda, Project Director*

Scope and Anticipated Number of Interviews

It usually is pretty easy to come up with a list of people to interview. Now is the time, however, to plan for the number of interviews you think a project can realistically complete. Although the temptation may be to recommend interviewing a long list of people, think this through carefully. Consider how many interviewers the project can expect to have, and be realistic about the number of interviews each interviewer can do. If your project is ongoing, set a specific internal goal. Unrealistically high goals for the number of interviews can, in a worst case scenario, burn out interviewers and make it difficult to complete a project.

 It takes about thirty hours to prepare for, conduct, and process an oral history interview.

Many planners recommend doing five to twelve fully processed (transcribed) interviews in a one-year period.[12] The number of fully-processed interviews that can realistically be completed depends on such factors as:

- the number of available, trained interviewers;
- the number of interviews each interviewer is expected to do;
- recording equipment availability;
- processing and transcribing availability; and
- project duration

Oral history interviews each take about thirty hours to prepare for, conduct, and process. An average interview lasts sixty to ninety minutes; the rest of this time is spent on preparation and processing, including transcribing. Generally, each volunteer interviewer, especially those new to oral history, can be expected to do between one and three fully processed interviews in a one-to-two year project.

Project Name

 A name gives a project an identity.

It's now time to recommend a project name. A name gives a project a distinct identity and helps communicate its purpose to the community. Include the name in the project plan, and indicate it should be used in all project correspondence and all contacts with community members and interviewees. When the project is completed, it will be used by the repository to identify the project and provide access to its interview information. Be creative if you wish, but make sure the name clearly identifies the project.

Examples of Community Oral History Project Names

- Oakland Chinatown Oral History Project
- Pioneers of the Medical Device Industry in Minnesota, 1995–2001
- Worcester Women's History Project–Oral History Initiative
- Greenwich Library Oral History Project
- India Association of Minnesota Oral History Project

Mission Statement

A mission statement spells out project name, goals, focus, and scope, and includes a statement saying the project is designed to adhere to oral history standards. Its development is a standard project planning step; in terms of decision-making process, it is based on and comes after discussions about focus, scope, and project name. Look for the mission statement at the top of the Project Design Statement. Once developed, it becomes the basic guide in planning and project design.

"Agreeing at the outset on what we wanted to accomplish— the mission—was important."

Susan Becker, From Secrecy to Accessibility: The Rocky Flats (CO) Nuclear Weapons Plant Oral Histories

Examples of Community Oral History Project Mission Statements

"Your Story and Mine: A Community of Hope" is a special program designed to give voice to transitional homeless, at-risk adults through oral history stories, art, poetry, photography and song in Lansing, Michigan. It has universal appeal—people learn to tell their stories and others learn to listen to them. While everyone has a story and no one can take that story away from an individual, we can provide opportunities for people to share their stories through—art, words, music, photographs and more. The program can be expanded and adapted to any group of people in any community in any part of the world.

"Your Story and Mine," Michigan Historical Museum,
Martha Aladjem Bloomfield, Project Director

To celebrate and document women's contributions to the history and social culture of Worcester and beyond.

Worcester (MA) Women's History Project, Oral History Initiative,
Lisa Krissoff Boehm, Project Consultant

The Greenwich Library Oral History Project exists to collect, preserve, and make available the personal recollections of people who have helped to make or lived through and observed the history of Greenwich, Connecticut.

Greenwich (CT) Library Oral History Project,
Catherine Ogden, Project Chair

Project mission statements vary in length and detail but all serve one basic purpose—to describe the project design for everyone involved in the project and for future users of the interview information. The preceding examples of mission statements are from respondents to the 2009 planning survey (see Appendix A). All of the examples include basic information; they illustrate the variety of mission statements project planners develop.

After the project planning team has recommended a mission statement, add it to the Project Design Statement as a definition of the proposed project design and include it in the project plan.

Figure 3.2. Reviewing interview content and names of potential interviewees for a project in the Ebb and Flow Oral History Program, County of Suffolk, England. Image © 2007 Theo Clarke

Project Interviewee List

Chances are, by this time, your planning team members have already started to think about names to include on a list of suggested project interviewees. In fact, many projects start with this step. But careful thought and consideration of proposed project goals, focus, scope, and mission statement are factors to consider here. At this planning stage, you may want to include more names on the list than will be included in the project, but be aware of project focus and scope as you develop the list. Keep your recommendations within your general scope guidelines, and unless you have defined a more narrow focus, include names representing multi-sided project content.

When identifying candidates for the interviewee list, consider the following criteria.

- have first-hand knowledge
- are able to communicate requested information
- have strong powers of observation
- are enthusiastic about participating
- are comfortable with being recorded

> "Identifying individuals to be interviewed and knowing why we wanted to interview each particular person was crucial."
>
> *Susan Becker, From Secrecy to Accessibility: The Rocky Flats (CO) Nuclear Weapons Plant Oral Histories*
>
> "When the project criteria were defined about whom to interview the process went smoother. (It was difficult to agree on who to include given so many potential candidates in the community!)"
>
> *The Azusa (CA) Heritage Project, Luisa Miranda, Project Director*

See **Volume 3,** *Managing a Community Oral History Project* and **Volume 4,** *Interviewing in Community Oral History*, for in-depth discussions about identifying and selecting interviewees. Look at the planning list as a beginning point, knowing it will be reviewed in detail during project management.

CHAPTER 4

Planning for People and Infrastructure

BEST PRACTICE NO. 2

Focus on oral history as a process.

BEST PRACTICE NO. 5

Make a plan.

BEST PRACTICE NO. 9

Process and archive all interview materials to preserve them for future use.

In this chapter, look for personnel guidelines, repository information, information about project forms, and project work space guidelines.

Team Member Options

Members of project teams carry out a project plan; identifying project team roles is a planning step. Regardless of whether your project is all-volunteer, all-paid, or a combination of the two, review the nearby checklist to determine team member options. For the most part, paid and volunteer community oral history projects have the same basic project team needs.

 One person may take on several oral history project team roles.

SUGGESTED ORAL HISTORY PROJECT TEAM ROLES

✓ project director

✓ interviewers

✓ transcribers

✓ recording technicians

✓ recorder maintenance technicians

✓ office support

✓ bookkeeper/accountant or fiscal sponsor

✓ processer/cataloger

Each role on the checklist is an important part of project team development. The most visible roles are the project director and interviewers. A project director can be an interviewer who takes on the extra duties of leading the project. In addition to doing the interviews, interviewers often help with or do the transcribing as well.

Project team roles also include office help, interview recording help and equipment maintenance, bookkeeping, and cataloging. These positions, although not as visible as the project director and interviewers, are necessary for project development. They probably will require less time than the more visible positions but should be recognized and included as part of the project team role recommendation in a project plan. See **Volume 3,** *Managing a Community Oral History Project,* for a detailed discussion of project team roles.

Repository Arrangements

Defining and recommending options for long-term preservation and access for oral history collections is a particularly important project planning step. The time to start planning for long-term care of your interview recordings is now. I'll provide the planning basics here; see **Volume 5,** *After the Interview in Community Oral History*, for a detailed discussion of this step from an archival viewpoint.

A *repository* is a facility that holds and maintains historical materials, including oral history project materials, and makes them available to others. Recommending a repository arrangement is a project planning team responsibility; options include libraries, archives, historical societies, museums, and digital repositories. Repositories may be existing places or places developed specifically to hold project materials. Some projects use web hosts

If your plans include project-supported website hosting, recommend budgeting for this beyond the life of the project.

with a cloud infrastructure, either as an in-house or commercial option, with built-in plans to meet long-term oral history preservation and access needs.

As you discuss interview preservation and access, think about the options. Do you want to be responsible for your project materials indefinitely or would you rather turn care and access over to someone else? If you intend to set up a project repository, here's an outline of what's involved at the planning stage. Review resources in the community to identify skilled archivists and others with the experience to set up and manage an oral history collection. Plan for time to research and develop a long-term preservation plan that covers recordings and transcripts. Check on availability and cost of storage that will provide permanent, ongoing preservation and access of project materials. If the project plans on including long-term web hosting, ask about disc space (the number of gigabytes available for project materials and possible future additions) and bandwidth (the number of gigabytes that can be sent and received in a specific period of time). See Appendix B for terminology and Appendix C for file size guides.

If you decide to use an existing repository, this too involves a series of planning steps. Begin by identifying potential repositories, and then meet with repository representatives to review basic organization and oral history policies.

CRITERIA TO LOOK FOR WHEN MAKING REPOSITORY DECISIONS

✓ institutional stability

✓ mission compatible with the project

✓ storage space

✓ environmental conditions needed to keep the project materials safe

✓ staff to process and catalog in a timely manner

✓ long-term preservation management plan
  Each of these points is important. Let's look at them more closely.

Institutional stability

Consider short-term and long-term needs for the oral histories. Ask about preservation policies and about policies and support for access and migration of recordings to keep up with technological advances.

Mission compatibility with your project

Look into compatibility between project focus and the collecting mission of a repository; ask about repository policies for oral histories covering your focus.

Storage space

To preserve oral histories, find adequate long-term storage space. Ask about short-term and long-term preservation and access options and data file size criteria. See Appendix C for audio and video file size guides.

Environmental conditions needed to keep the project materials safe

Optimum archival conditions contribute to long-term preservation of recordings. An archive should meet current standards; web hosts should be able to show evidence of long-term stability.

Staff to process and catalog in a timely manner

As anyone working in a library or historical organization can testify, a donation consisting of hours of interview recordings and hundreds of pages of transcripts can be a challenge to catalog; an organized set of descriptive information is helpful to repository staff. In addition, ask about available staff to process and catalog oral history materials. Many institutions have experienced cutbacks in funding and staff and may not have the people or time to catalog oral histories.

Long-term preservation management plan

Long-term preservation of oral histories is an ethical commitment. Review the preservation plan of the repositories and ask about how interviews recorded in outdated technologies are handled.

Most repositories have specific criteria for acquiring new collections, based on the relevance of the materials to their existing collections, the condition of the materials, and the available staff and physical space to accommodate them. Oral histories are unique in a number of ways and often baffle curators. For this reason it is important to contact potential repositories early in the planning stage, and set up a dialog, so that each party thoroughly understands the responsibilities and expectations of the other.

If you decide to work with a repository, be prepared for questions. Before meeting with anyone, request and review information about their oral history policies.

Sample Oral History Accession Repository Guidelines

Repositories often require oral history collections to have:

- a signed and dated Legal Release Agreement for each interview,
- recordings done on production-quality equipment,
- interviews that show evidence of careful project planning,
- full interview transcripts, and
- cataloging information, including name of interviewer, name of interviewee, date and place of interview, topics discussed during the interview, and the spelling of proper and place names mentioned in the interview.

You may have several false starts before identifying one or more appropriate repositories. Sometimes repositories, no matter how supportive their personnel are of oral history, cannot accept interviews. A project scope and mission may be outside their designated collecting area, they may not be set up to handle recording media on an ongoing basis, or they may not have time to do the cataloging needed to make the information accessible. Think carefully about all the options. Do your homework and be prepared to explain why and how a project would add to a repository's collections.

Begin to contact repositories early in the planning process. Consider the following in a project plan.

- Repository representatives may want to review recommended recording formats. Some repositories have the capability of working with video, whereas others may be better suited to working only with audio recordings.

- Repositories often have specific guidelines which they will ask you to incorporate into a project plan. This could include wording for a Legal Release Agreement or guidelines for transcribing formats.

- Repositories may have specific requirements about the types of information that must be turned in with oral history collections to facilitate cataloging.

- Repositories may have specific guidelines about how oral histories are accessed.

WHAT ORAL HISTORY PLANNING DIRECTORS NEED TO KNOW ABOUT A REPOSITORY

✓ Has the repository accepted donations of oral histories in the past?

✓ How well do the interview focus and topics fit with the collecting mission of the repository?

✓ What kinds of oral history materials does the repository accept? Recording media? Transcripts? Both?

✓ What kinds of recording media does the repository accept? Analog audio or video? Digital audio or video? None or all of these?

✓ Does the repository have a preservation plan for recording media?

✓ What is the repository policy on ownership and copyright?

✓ Does the repository have a recommended oral history Legal Release Agreement or recommended language for a Legal Release Agreement?

✓ What is the policy for access of materials to researchers?

✓ How will the oral histories be cataloged?

✓ What is the estimated timeframe for making the oral histories accessible to users?

✓ What kind of online access does the repository provide?

WHAT REPOSITORY REPRESENTATIVES NEED TO KNOW ABOUT ORAL HISTORY PROJECTS

✓ What are the oral history project interview topics and how well do they fit with the repository's collecting mission?

✓ What is the size and extent of collection: number of interviews; number of physical items (discs, transcripts, photos, digital files)?

✓ In what formats will the oral histories be delivered? Transcripts? Audio or video discs? Digital files?

✓ What metadata—the data or information about the oral histories—will be provided for cataloging?

✓ What is the delivery schedule? Will items be deposited at once or in phases? Is this a one-time only or an ongoing relationship with the repository?

✓ Are there any outstanding legal issues or unsigned Legal Release Agreements?

Once project planners and repository representatives come to an understanding about oral history project materials, it's time to develop a Letter of Agreement for Repository. This formally defines the arrangement by spelling out the responsibilities of all parties involved; it is a helpful guide for community oral history projects in meeting oral history preservation and access goals. As with all suggested community oral history project forms, this form is not long or detailed, but it clearly identifies everyone's responsibilities (see Figure 4.1, below).

LETTER OF AGREEMENT FOR REPOSITORY

This letter summarizes the responsibilities of the _____ (repository) and the _____ (oral history project). In addition to this document, a Legal Release Agreement form signed by each interviewer and interviewee will accompany each oral history.

The _____ **oral history project** is responsible for the following tasks and for the costs incurred:

- Prepare audio- or video-recorded interviews in formats and quality determined by repository
- Transcribe oral history interviews according to style guidelines provided by repository
- Deliver signed Legal Release Agreement for each interview
- Deliver transcript and discs in format agreed upon.

The _____ **repository** is responsible for the following tasks and for the costs incurred:

- Advise in selection and training of interviewers
- Advise in development of project plan
- Catalog oral histories for local catalog and WorldCat
- Format, copy, and bind oral history materials
- Make copies available for use according to repository's access policy.

Number of interviews _____

Timeframe for delivery _____

Number of copies of each interview _____

REPOSITORY	ORAL HISTORY PROJECT
Name (print) _____	Name (print) _____
Signature _____	Signature _____
Title_____	Title_____
Date_____	Date_____

Figure 4.1. Letter of Agreement for Repository

"The [project] had originally planned to archive its own interviews, but had not gotten very far in the process and had little expertise in the area. Once the ... oral history committee became aware of the extensive archives already in existence at the MROHP, [Maria Rogers Oral History Project] and the program's willingness to collaborate ... in archiving oral histories collected by its interviewers, we moved quickly to reach an agreement to have the MROHP archive the interviews collected under the auspices of the museum. The relationship has been extremely fruitful—in all likelihood, we would still be trying to locate the funding and expertise to archive our interviews online and the public would have very little access to the information. The collaboration with the MROHP has allowed tremendous public access to our interviews, and helped to raise the profile of the museum and the oral history project."

Hannah Nordhaus/Susan Becker, From Secrecy to Accessibility: The Rocky Flats (CO) Nuclear Weapons Plant Oral Histories

Notice that the form has a place to include the number of interviews, the deadline for project delivery, and the number of copies that will be turned over to the repository. This information is based on decisions (see Chapter 3 and the Project Design Statement) made by project planning team members and discussions with a designated repository. Project plans often recommend repository options with the understanding that management teams will make a final decision; particulars on this form provide an example of the types of arrangements that can be made.

 Use the planning process to make sure you have a permanent home for oral history interviews. They are your most valuable project products.

The Internet

Although repositories are essential for ongoing preservation and access for oral histories, the Internet can provide additional online access options—either by working with a repository or through a project's own web page.

The Internet is a website access tool; a website is not a permanent repository.

The Internet, however, also can pose specific ethical and legal questions for oral historians. When planning a project, review the implications of Internet access from the viewpoints of the interviewee, interviewer, project, and community. Discuss various options—a web page may be used to provide information about your project or, more broadly, to provide access to recordings and transcripts. Consider the use of social networking sites and how they could benefit your project. Think about your project goals and the nature of the community and be prepared to answer questions about worldwide access. The Internet is a widely-used tool; just make sure your project plans are clear about how best to use it for your community and your project. Review the points on the nearby checklist as you discuss this part of a project plan.

CONSIDERATIONS FOR POSSIBLE ONLINE ACCESS

✓ Why are we interested in online access for our interviews?

✓ What exactly will be accomplished by online access? What additional communities will be served?

✓ Who will host the oral histories? Will the project create its own website or will project materials be deposited in an existing repository? What is the existing repository's online access policy?

✓ Will the online access be temporary or ongoing? Who will set up the website? Who will maintain it? What will it cost?

✓ Will there be a gate-keeping step, such as a user agreement, involved before proceeding to the viewing page? If so, how will this work?

✓ Does the Legal Release Agreement clearly give an interviewee's permission to post an interview on the Internet?

✓ What are the ethical implications of making sure an interviewee understands what it means to have online access to the interview?

It's also helpful to understand the options available for online access on the Internet. You can allow for varying levels of access in a number of ways: you can suggest that an existing repository add a page to its web presence; you can plan on working with a digital library to post interviews or excerpts online; or you can include plans to develop and post project web page portfolios containing interview information, analysis of information, and illustrations. You may also find your project can contribute to an aggregation of oral histories on a common topic. (See, for example, the Hurricane Digital Memory Bank or the Veterans Oral History Project: A Project of the American Folklife Center at the Library of Congress.)

Here are some examples that illustrate various Internet access options.

- **Post catalog records online.** This facilitates user requests to repository reference staff but limits researchers to on-site use or works with another provider for Internet access. See, for example, the Minnesota Historical Society (http://www.mnhs.org/collections/oralhistory/oralhistory. htm), Montana Historical Society (http://mhs.mt.gov/research/ MTMemoryProj.asp), the Northeast Minnesota Historical Center (http://libguides.d.umn.edu/nemhc) archival collections, working with the Minnesota Digital Library (http://www.mndigital.org/) for access.

- **Provide a mixture of on-site and online access.** See, for example, the Maria Rogers Oral History Program at the Carnegie Branch Library for Local History website (http://boulderlibrary.org/carnegie/ collections/mrohp.html) and the Oakland Chinatown Oral History Project website (http://memorymap.oacc.cc/). In each of these, the repository provides access to oral history collections onsite and through a searchable digital archive via the Internet that is linked to the public library catalog. The repositories also have developed links to oral history videos and podcasts through social media connections.

- **Develop a digital archive for oral history interview access.** See the Densho Digital Archive, the archive for Densho: The Japanese American Legacy Project (http://www.densho.org/), as an example. In this project-developed archive, all interviews are fully transcribed, segmented for ease of viewing, and keyword searchable.

The Internet is a powerful tool for oral historians. But always remember it is a tool, not a place for a permanent project repository.

Forms and Record Keeping

Record keeping helps keep an oral history project organized. Three of the suggested project forms—a Project Design Statement, Legal Release Agreement, and Letter of Agreement for Repository—have been discussed already. The forms covered here help document interview context and maintain preliminary access to interview information. Using these forms as a guide, the project planning team should adapt and recommend record-keeping forms and procedures.

A complete set of *Toolkit* forms is included in **Volume 1,** *Introduction to Community Oral History,* and online at www.LCoastPress.com. Review the descriptions of the forms and determine what will work for your project.

RECOMMENDED ORAL HISTORY PROJECT PLANNING FORMS

- ✓ Project Design Statement
- ✓ Legal Release Agreement
- ✓ Interviewee Recommendation Form
- ✓ Interviewee Biographical Profile
- ✓ Interview Summary
- ✓ Interview Tracking Form
- ✓ Letter of Agreement for Interviewer
- ✓ Letter of Agreement for Repository
- ✓ Letter of Agreement for Transcriber
- ✓ Photograph and Memorabilia Receipt

As discussed earlier, the Project Design Statement is the master project form. Use it to document project planning team decisions; its use indicates acceptance of these decisions by everyone involved with a project (see Chapter 3). The Legal Release Agreement transfers rights from the interviewer and interviewee to a designated repository or project archive (see Chapter 2).

An Interviewee Recommendation Form helps with interviewee selection. Use a form like this to assemble information about suggested interviewees and document action taken (see Figure 4.2).

An Interviewee Biographical Profile provides background on interviewees chosen for a project. The information on this form can help an interviewer prepare for an interview; it also adds to an understanding of interview context. Develop and use a biographical profile form that meets the needs of your project (see Figure 4.3).

An Interview Summary form documents interview content and context; the information on it can be used to take preliminary control over the content of the interviews, as well as to help in transcribing and developing cataloging records (see Figure 4.4). The form lists the project name followed by the interviewee's name as it appears in public records for organization and cataloging purposes. Underneath the name, project medium and technical materials sections provide technological control over the interview. The next section, interview notes, provides a place to add contextual information; the proper names and keywords section is helpful for transcribing purposes and for cataloging.

INTERVIEWEE RECOMMENDATION FORM	
PROJECT NAME	
NAME	**CONTACT**
PLACE OF RESIDENCE	**DATE OF BIRTH**
RELEVANCE TO THE PROJECT (How will this person's life history relate to the goals of the project?)	
BIOGRAPHICAL SUMMARY (family, education, professional experience, and community activities, as relating to the project)	
RECOMMENDED BY	**CONTACT**
ACTION	
_____ *Approved* _____ *Not Approved*	***INITIAL MEETING DATE***
INTERVIEWER	
INTERVIEW DATE AND LOCATION	

Figure 4.2. Interviewee Recommendation Form

INTERVIEWEE BIOGRAPHICAL PROFILE	
PROJECT NAME	
NAME	CONTACT
OTHER NAMES KNOWN BY	DATE/PLACE OF BIRTH
PLACE OF RESIDENCE	YEARS IN THE COMMUNITY
OCCUPATION	EDUCATION
RELEVANCE TO THE PROJECT	
RELEVANT BIOGRAPHICAL INFORMATION (AS IT RELATES TO THE GOALS OF THE PROJECT)	
FAMILY (full name, date of birth, relationship to interviewee)	
FRIENDS AND ASSOCIATES (full name, date of birth, relationship to interviewee)	
PLACES TRAVELED OR LIVED	
COMMUNITY ACTIVITIES (Include activity, date, and significance to the project)	
INTERESTS	
INFLUENCES	
LIFE MILESTONES	
Completed by	Date

Figure 4.3. Interviewee Biographical Profile

INTERVIEW SUMMARY	
PROJECT NAME	**INTERVIEW ID#**
INTERVIEWEE	**INTERVIEWER**
NAME (as it will appear in the public record)	**NAME**
CONTACT	**CONTACT**
OTHER NAMES KNOWN BY	
INTERVIEW DATE	**INTERVIEW LENGTH**
RECORDING MEDIUM _____digital audio _____digital video	
DELIVERY MEDIUM _____sound file _____sound card _____CD _____DVD	
TECHNICAL NOTES (make/model of recorder, format recorded, microphone notes)	
INTERVIEW NOTES (physical environment, interviewee's mood, people or animals in the room, interruptions)	
DATE LEGAL RELEASE AGREEMENT SIGNED _____	
PROPER NAMES AND KEYWORDS (personal and place names with proper spelling, dates, and keywords)	
SUMMARY OF INTERVIEW CONTENT	
COMPLETED BY	**DATE**

Figure 4.4. Interview Summary Form

The Interview Tracking Form lists project responsibilities for after-inter-view care—all the tasks that turn an interview recording into a finished oral history—and provides a process for internal control over the responsibilities (see Figure 4.5). Use a form like this, along with the Letter of Agreement for

INTERVIEW TRACKING FORM			
PROJECT NAME		INTERVIEW ID#	
INTERVIEWEE		INTERVIEWER	
NAME		NAME	
CONTACT		CONTACT	
INTERVIEW DATE			
DATE COMPLETED	TASK	NOTES	
	Log interview recording and assign an interview ID#		
	Log *Legal Release Agreement*		
	Log *Interview Summary*		
	Copy recording		
	Label recording media		
	Transcribe interview		
	Audit-check transcript		
	Check facts and verify spelling of proper names		
	Get interviewee's approval of transcript		
	Complete *Cataloging Work Sheet*		
	Assemble materials for repository		
	Deliver completed oral history to repository		
	Prepare oral history for website		
	Thank Interviewee		
	Archive master files		

Figure 4.5. Interview Tracking Form

Repository (see Figure 4.1) to recommend coordinating tasks and clarify af-ter-interview responsibilities and track their progress. Project planners may decide to recommend tracking these steps on a spreadsheet rather than this style of a form.

Increasingly, interviewers, equipment operators, and transcribers are asked to sign Letters of Agreement (also called Letters of Understanding) outlining project team member responsibilities. These are distinguished from the Letter of Agreement for Repository (see Figure 4.1), which defines the commitments of oral history project and repository personnel. The examples here are for interviewers and transcribers (see Figures 4.6 and 4.7).

LETTER OF AGREEMENT FOR INTERVIEWER

I, _____, an interviewer for the _____ Oral History Project, understand and agree to the following.

- I understand the goals and purposes of this project and understand I represent the oral history project when I am conducting an interview.

- I will participate in an oral history interviewer training workshop.

- I understand the legal and ethical considerations regarding the interviews and will communicate them to and carry them out with each person I interview.

- I am willing to do the necessary preparation, including background research, for each interview I conduct.

- I will treat each interviewee with respect, and I understand each interview will be conducted in a spirit of openness that will allow each interviewee to answer all questions as fully and freely as he or she wishes.

- I am aware of the need for confidentiality of interview content until such time as the interviews are released for public use per the repository's guidelines, and I will not exploit the interviewee's story.

- I understand my responsibilities regarding any archival materials or artifacts related to the interview that the interviewee may want to include in the interview process.

- I agree to turn all interview materials over to the repository in a timely manner and to help facilitate all necessary processing and cataloging steps.

INTERVIEWER	ORAL HISTORY PROJECT
Name (print) _____	Name (print) _____
Signature _____	Signature _____
Date _____	Date _____

Figure 4.6. Letter of Agreement for Interviewer

LETTER OF AGREEMENT FOR TRANSCRIBER

I, _____ (transcriber), agree to the following:

- Create a verbatim transcript according to style guide provided
- Clearly indicate the interviewee, interviewer, and place and date of the interview at the head of the transcript according to the style guide provided
- Deliver electronic copy in a Microsoft Word 2010 or later document
- Timeframe for delivery _____

The transcription process will include (check all that apply):

_____ Audit-checking the transcript

_____ A reasonable amount of research for correct spelling of proper names

_____ Creating chapter headings

_____ Creating a Table of Contents

_____ Creating an index

_____ Other (Specify) _____

The oral history project will provide a list of proper and place names wherever possible to facilitate accurate transcribing.

As transcriber, I understand that all information contained in the transcript is confidential. I agree not to disclose any information contained in the transcript, nor will I allow anyone access to the recording or the electronic files while they are in my possession. I agree to delete electronic files and destroy discs at the instruction of the oral history project or at the conclusion of the assignment.

TRANSCRIBER	ORAL HISTORY PROJECT
Name (print) _____	Name (print) _____
Signature _____	Signature _____
Title_____	Title_____
Date_____	Date_____

Figure 4.7. Letter of Agreement for Transcriber

Letters of Agreement list the ethical and project performance expectations for team members. Project planners could recommend a similar form for videographers and other team members as well.

In their contact with interviewees, oral history interviewers often learn about historical photographs, diaries, letters, and other memorabilia. Sometimes interviewees offer these items to a project. Recommend use of a Photograph and Memorabilia Receipt to help everyone keep track of this material until decisions are made on what to do with it (see Figure 4.8).

PHOTOGRAPH AND MEMORABILIA RECEIPT	
PROJECT NAME	
OWNER	
Name	
Address	Phone/Email
ITEM	
Type	Quantity
Detailed Description (Describe item and circumstances of loan)	
Associated Dates	
Physical Condition	
Instructions for use:	
RETURNED	
Items returned by (name):	

OWNER	INTERVIEWER
Name (print)	Name (print)
Signature	Signature
Date	Date

Figure 4.8. Photograph and Memorabilia Receipt

Using these forms as a guide, include the development and use of forms in your project plan. They document information that will become part of your permanent project records. For more information, see **Volume 3,** *Managing a Community Oral History Project* and **Volume 5,** *After the Interview in Community Oral History.*

Work Space Needs

Does this story sound familiar? You are a member of an organization that is careful about maintaining its files. But the organization's files are stored under the bed in the president's or secretary's guest room. Because yours is an oral history project, you have recordings, which take up space on your computer. Forms take up more space in the file cabinets of another member. And where does the organization store the recorders and other project equipment when not in use? Who runs an equipment check-out system? The oral history seed is fast becoming a sapling and soon will be a tree. Now is the time to start planning for space needs.

Oral history projects have several basic space needs—interviewing space and work space with room for storage. Oral history interviewing space may be an office or public meeting room; this will depend on the type of recording equipment used and decisions about where to do the interviews. Projects using video recorders may need a more formal interviewing space than those using audio recorders. Interview location decisions also often depend on the interviewee preference for conducting the interview at home or in a designated project site. Look for interviewing space that meets the following criteria at a minimum.

- Ambient sound can be controlled as much as possible.
- Access during interview can be controlled.
- Space is accessible to interviewees.
- Space is comfortable for interviewees.
- Setting up audio and video recorder is manageable.
- Setting is suitable for video.

Ambient sound is background noise, such as running air conditioners or humming refrigerators, that people often tune out but recorders always pick up. Plan to look for interviewing space with as much control over ambient sound as possible. Interviewee accessibility and comfort also are important factors as are manageable places to put a recorder and options for suitable

Figure 4.9. Meeting room with planning space at the Minnesota Historical Society, St Paul, MN. Image © Barb Sommer

video settings. Meeting rooms of local libraries, historical societies, and community centers are good options to consider. See **Volume 4,** *Interviewing in Community Oral History*, for detailed information about interviewing space needs and apply the information as needed to your planning decisions about project interviewing space.

Work space may be just a desk, chair, work table, and file cabinet—a place to store project records and hold meetings. Rather than turn your living room into oral history central, explore the possibility that a community supporter, local historical society, or local library may be able to make office space and storage space available. The space doesn't have to be large but should be accessible to project planners and supporters. If it's too small for meetings, try and find a location that has access to a meeting room.

Look for work space with access to phones, fax, photocopying, and the Internet. Recommend acquiring a desk, chair, and file cabinet for basic work needs, as well as a computer with enough dedicated space to hold project recordings. And, don't forget to list office supplies including paper, a letterhead with the project name on it, postage, and acid-free paper for transcripts in infrastructure recommendations.

Interviewing and work space can be purchased, loaned, or donated. If loaned or donated, keep track of the gift. Determine its value for the project budget and acknowledge it.

CHAPTER 5

Equipment Planning

BEST PRACTICE NO. 5

Make a plan.

BEST PRACTICE NO. 6

Choose appropriate technology with an eye toward
present and future needs.

Oral history is technology based, and equipment decisions are a central part of the planning process. This includes more than recording equipment, although recorders are the equipment item most commonly discussed among oral historians. Oral history practitioners also use computer equipment for maintaining records, doing and storing transcripts, and storing sound and video files. This chapter starts by examining equipment planning options. It then covers recording equipment accessories and other equipment suggestions. I've included supporting information in two appendices—Appendix B: Equipment and Technology Terms and Appendix C: Recording Equipment Standards.

The nearby checklist sets out some of the most frequently asked questions about oral history recording equipment. Review the mission statement, project focus and scope, and the Project Design Statement as you talk through answers to these questions. All will help determine recording equipment recommendations that will work best for your project and your community.

ORAL HISTORY PROJECT EQUIPMENT FAQS

✓ Do we want to record interviews as audio or video or both? Why?

✓ Do we plan to use equipment we already have, or will we borrow equipment, purchase equipment, or outsource recording?

✓ What technical support expertise do we need, and how can we find it in the community?

✓ What are our electronic storage options?

✓ How will we handle transcribing?

✓ What will this part of the project cost?

Technology changes, but the underlying concepts that guide oral history recording equipment decisions remain the same. Maximize the quality of oral history recordings by using the best equipment you can find. Recording equipment made for broad consumer use often utilizes cheaper parts; this can result in poorer quality recordings.

Recorders

First—the big question—will you record in audio or video or both and why? Oral history project planners face this question almost as soon as they start talking about doing a project. The answer will depend on why you are doing the project, how you want to use the interviews, and what long-term plans are for preserving and providing access to them. If you are primarily interested in interview content and don't think a visual setting or documentation of non-verbal communication will further project goals, consider recording in audio. The recorders are easy to use, the data files are comparatively small, and they record in non-proprietary cross-platform uncompressed formats that are relatively easy to manage for long-term storage. If, however, you will need visuals of interviews or you want to document visual settings (beyond a still photograph) or both verbal and non-verbal communication, use video. The interviewing process with video is more complicated, but you will have the added advantage of both an audio and a visual recording.

Review the pros and cons of audio and video recording (see Table 5.1) as you discuss this planning step. Don't be driven to use one or another type of recorder simply to keep up with the latest technology; recommend equipment that helps achieve your goals and mission.[13]

Audio recorders are a long-time oral history standard, although technological advances have resulted in increased use of video recorders. Both

Audio and Video Recorder Planning Guide

	Pros	*Cons*
Audio	Easy to use	Does not record visual setting in video (though taking a still photograph of an interviewee in an interview setting can document visual interview context)
	Records in non-proprietary, uncompressed format – an oral history standard	Does not record non-verbal communication
	Uncompressed files are a manageable storage size	Lack of visual can limit long-term use options for recording
	Records in broadcast quality	
	Interview settings less formal	
	Files can be compressed into MPEG format to put on the Internet	
Video	Records in high definition	Recording specifications not yet standardized
	Records visual of interviewee in interview setting	Uncompressed files too large for effective long-term storage
	Records verbal and non-verbal communication	Additional equipment is needed to record an interview
	Visual can expand programmatic uses of recording	Can include added personnel needs such as videographer
		Additional training needed
		Interview setting more formal
		Video data files require much larger and more complex storage needs than audio data files

Table 5.1. Pros and cons of audio and video recording

audio and video meet accepted oral history standards. To achieve high-quality sound and video and to help maximize ongoing user options, work with the best quality equipment you can find. This doesn't mean using the fanciest equipment on the market, but means equipment with high-quality component parts.

Audio Recorders

If using audio, you will have several types of recorders to choose from. The most common are solid state recorders, which record in high quality sound on removable, reusable compact flash (CF) or secure digital (SD) memory cards. You also will find hard disc drive recorders, computers with a microphone input, and direct-to-computer recorders. This last type of recorder requires a computer and an audio interface (A/D converter), unless a microphone input is built in to the computer. It does not always produce high quality recordings because of fans and other sounds, but it avoids the need to download a recording onto a computer to save it.

SPECIFICATIONS TO LOOK FOR WHEN CHOOSING AUDIO RECORDING EQUIPMENT

✓ is relatively easy to operate

✓ has a short learning curve

✓ is sturdy

✓ is readily available

✓ uses solid state technology

✓ has an external microphone input and headphone jack

✓ produces CD quality files or better

✓ records in non-proprietary format, cross-platform uncompressed format

✓ is capable of generating metadata

✓ uses an AC adapter

Audio recorders recommended for oral history use are solid-state with the capability of recording on a removable memory card. They should create, at a minimum, uncompressed (file extension .wav or .aiff) CD (16 bit/44.1 kHz) quality files or better. See Appendix C for detailed information.

Video Recorders

Most video recorders have good immediate recording quality. However, they are subject to rapid technology changes and technological obsolescence. Although some may cost less and be widely available, especially those manufactured for home or consumer-grade use, they are not as durable.

SPECIFICATIONS TO LOOK FOR WHEN CHOOSING VIDEO RECORDING EQUIPMENT

✓ is relatively easy to operate

✓ has a short learning curve

✓ is sturdy

✓ availability

✓ is solid state

✓ produces HD quality files

✓ has an external microphone input and headphone jack

✓ uses an AC adaptor

The most common video recorders used by oral historians record high definition (HD) onto either an internal hard drive or removable, reusable memory cards. As of the date of this publication, the most common and desirable recording format among consumer- and prosumer-grade video recorders is Advanced Video Coding High Definition (AVCHD). The important characteristics of video recorder settings are compression, and resolution and frame rate. All video recordings utilize some form of compression in order to capture and store data efficiently. AVCHD uses a form of H.264/MPEG4 compression, but the recorders often have several quality settings and should be set to highest possible recording quality the camera will allow. Most HD cameras will also record in several different resolutions and frame rates. The best approach is to use the highest resolution and frame rate the camera will record, even though this will require the largest amount of storage. The most desirable resolutions and frame rates are 1920x1080 60p, 30p, or 60i, or 1280x720 60p resolution.[14] See Appendix C for more information.

RECORDERS SUMMARY

✓ Think about audio and visual communication—the power of voice and the power of visual; recommend equipment that meets project interview focus and scope and will best serve your needs.

✓ If capturing visual context is important, consider the setting and interviewee background in the composition of the frame.

✓ There is no one "best" equipment choice. Recording equipment is an interviewing tool. Recommend equipment that can easily be used by project interviewers.

✓ Consider practical issues, such as cost or access to borrowed or leased equipment.

If the recommendation is to use video, remember video data files are much larger than audio data files. Because video recordings require more storage and web hosting space and are more complicated to preserve for future access, anticipating these needs and making recommendations on how to handle them are critical planning steps.

Whether you use audio or video, don't lose sight of your first and primary purpose, which is to collect information from the community in file formats that support high-quality recording, preservation, and ongoing access to the complete and full set of interviews. Your responsibility as oral history planners is to recommend recording equipment that supports the project's goals, mission, and focus.

Microphones

Microphones are another important part of the oral history equipment package. To maximize sound quality, oral historians use insulated external microphones. An external microphone, as opposed to one that is built-in, minimizes equipment noise and provides flexibility in recorder placement. When choosing microphones, consider type, number of channels, and sound pick-up patterns. If you will be recording outdoors, look into using a microphone with protection against environmental noises such as wind.

Use a microphone that picks up all voices in an interview. Sound quality also is important but, unless the project has special interviewing circumstances, a microphone manufactured for music recording is not needed. Oral historians commonly work with a sturdy, rugged, dynamic, omnidirectional, mono or stereo single-stand microphone or directional lavaliere clip-on microphones—one for each interview participant. Appendix C gives my rec-ommended specifications for microphones and other equipment.

Accessories

Audio or video recording equipment isn't enough on its own: you'll need ac-cessories to help store the spoken words and make their quality the best pos-sible for preservation and access. If using hard discs or memory cards, opt for removable cards with enough storage space to meet interviewing needs.

Other recording equipment accessories to consider are:

■ headphones to monitor sound level and recording quality during the interview,

■ cables and connectors that are long enough to allow for maximum flexibility in positioning the recorder and are shielded to reduce interference, and

■ a USB cable or card reader to transfer recording from a recorder to a computer hard drive.

If you're using video recording and your budget will allow it, the fol-lowing additional, optional accessories will help improve the quality of your final product:

■ a tripod to balance the camera and assure a steady (rather than shaky hand-held) video,

■ a light kit and/or a reflector that can be mounted on a stand to increase and control light, and

■ a video monitor to review video recording quality during an interview.

Computers and External Hard Drives

Computers and external hard drives usually are crucial both for informa-tion processing and providing recording and project administrative storage. Again, see Appendix C for details of what to look for when selecting this equipment for these uses.

Computers also can be used as recording devices. Discussions about the use of Gizmo, Skype, and Audacity, among others, often come up, especially for long-distance interviews. Interviewers also ask about recording on smart phones. What are the questions for planners to consider when reviewing these options? Ask yourselves the following questions.

- What are your reasons for considering any of these options?

- What recording software or apps does each use and in what ways does each meet basic oral history recording standards? Is the software non-proprietary and are the recordings commonly accessible?

- What is the sound and/or visual recording quality of the option you are considering? If the recording is in audio, is the option to record in an uncompressed format available?

- What training is needed to use these options and who is available to provide the training?

- What are the repository criteria for recordings using these options?

- What is the process for preserving the recordings and making them accessible?

As you review and discuss your answers to these questions, consider the full impact your decision will have on project interviews. An interview may sound good when recorded, but if the recording was made using software not designed for long-term preservation and access, it may not retain sound quality or accessibility. Always plan for the needs of your project now and in the future. The Oral History listserv, H-Oralhist, is a helpful source of information about changes in all aspects of recording technology, including use of computers and smartphones as recorders. Access it at http://www.h-net.org/~oralhist/.

 Plan for the equipment needs of your project now and into the future.

Transcribing Equipment

Oral historians work with a single-preservation file format that is commonly available and, if possible, is open source, cross-platform, and readily searchable and retains formatting if conversion is needed. A transcribing-equipment set includes a computer equipped with a transcribing program and a headset and foot pedal plugged in to the computer through a USB port. Look for software that works with your computer and data files.

Technology in the 21st century is a moving target of innovation, experimentation, and commerce-driven equipment choices. As oral historians we use this ever-changing technology to record interviews. In your project plan, recommend recorders that meet project design needs. For details and updates on information in this chapter, consult experts in your own area or the Oral History Association (OHA) technology resources website (http://www.oralhistory.org/technology/).

CHAPTER 6

All About Money

BEST PRACTICE NO. 2

Focus on oral history as a process.

BEST PRACTICE NO. 5

Make a plan.

Oral history projects deal with value—not just in the information recorded but in the materials needed to do the recordings. This is as true for all-volunteer projects as for projects with grant funding and institutional support.

Developing a budget—matching spending with support—is a key part of oral history project planning. There are many ways numbers can be shifted within a budget, but in the end the bottom line—the balance—must be very close to zero. It's as simple as this:

$$\text{Expenses} > \text{Income} = \text{Bad}$$

$$\text{Expenses} < (\text{or equal to}) \text{ Income} = \text{Good}$$

Budget planning is part of the oral history project planning process. This chapter will identify project financial needs, review a sample (fictitious) project budget, and identify ways to meet possible project expenses.

Let's start with a couple of basic guidelines.

- As you develop a budget, keep the recommended project design uppermost in mind; resist the temptation to add options as you go along.
- Keep the figures for oral history project design separate from those for project products; develop separate budgets for project events and activities, such as websites, documentaries, exhibits, and publications.

I've provided a list of budget-related definitions in Appendix D. If you have any questions about the terms used in this chapter, check this list.

Project Budget

Some of the most common oral history project questions are about money. How much will a project, even an all-volunteer one, really cost? Where can projects find funding or other types of support? These are not easily-answered questions, but there is information that can help. Let's start with a look at a proposed project budget outline.

Project Budget Categories

Budget items generally fall in one of the following three categories.

- one-time or non-recurring expenses
- overhead cost
- per-interview costs

Each of these categories focuses on a specific area of community oral history project needs. *One-time costs* cover some of the most expensive project items. *Overhead costs* include office equipment, office space, and office supplies. *Interview costs* cover the cost of doing a project interview. Put together they add up to total project cost or value.

ORAL HISTORY PROJECT BUDGET OUTLINE

One-time or non-recurring expenses

✓ recording equipment, including carrying case
✓ microphone and accessories, including cables
✓ computer
✓ external hard drive(s)
✓ transcribing equipment and accessories

Overhead costs

✓   consultant fees (if needed)

✓   project team payment or reimbursement (if needed)

✓   equipment maintenance and repair

✓   interviewer and transcriber training workshops

✓   interviewer and administrative space value or cost

✓   photocopy, postage, telephone, fax, and office supplies

✓   project orientation packets

✓   interviewer and transcriber training manuals

Per-interview costs

✓   value of time for interview-related research

✓   interview media

✓   long-term electronic storage (web hosting) space (if costs incurred)

✓   interviewer fee or donated value

✓   transcriber fee or donated value

✓   videographer fee or donated value

✓   printed and bound copy of transcript for interviewee

✓   copy of recording for interviewee (optional)

✓   travel

Budget Discussion

These budget categories are linked to the oral history planning steps. Taken together, with per-interview costs multiplied by the number of planned project interviews, items within these categories represent the total projected cost or value of a community oral history project. As part of a project plan, identify possible project income and potential expenses and make recommendations about how to handle them. Use the sample (fictitious) budget in Table 6.1 as a template for project planning.

Project planning teams sometimes develop several budget options, ranging from a budget reflecting minimal project support to one at a more well-funded level. Doing this can help you think through your project priorities, making sure basics are covered first. It also can help you identify areas of potential project expansion, if more funding or support becomes available.

Sample (Fictitious) Oral History Project Budget						
	January	February	March	April	May	Total
Income by Source						
Grants	2,975					2,975
Donations						
Cash	120	85	75	185	50	615
In-Kind	5,280	5,280	5,255	5,255	5,280	25,600
Volunteer	2,000	2,000	2,000	2,000	2,000	10,000
TOTAL	10,225	7,315	7,180	7,290	7,180	39,940
Expenses by Type						
One-Time						
Computer	645					645
Recorder /Accessories		690				690
External Hard Drive, 2@$60				120		120
Overhead						
Office 50sq.ft @$100/sq.ft	5,000	5,000	5,000	5,000	5,000	25,000
Bookkeeping 2hr@$50/hr	100	100	100	100	100	500
Office Help 2hr@$25/hr	50	50	50	50	50	250
Office Supplies	50	50	25	25	50	200
Phtcpy/Pstge	35	35	35	35	35	175
Phone/Fax	45	45	45	45	45	225
Project Packet	45					45
Workshops Meeting Costs 2@$75	75		75			150
Manuals $35/mtg	35		35			70
Ldr. Honorarium	100		100		200	
Per-Interview						
Interviewers 40hrs@$50/hr	2,000	2,000	2,000	2,000	2,000	10,000
Transcribing $50/interview hr			400	400	400	1,200
Recording Media 3@$40		80	40			120
Travel @$.55/mile						
Pres/Access Copies	25	25	25	25	25	125
Interviewee Copies	25	25	25	25	25	125
TOTAL	$8,255	$8,125	$7,980	$7,850	$7,730	$39,940

Table 6.1. Sample (Fictitious) Oral History Project Budget

"We used state and community grants and the organization's own fund-raising efforts."

Worcester (MA) Women's History Project, Oral History Initiative, Lisa Krissoff Boehm, Project Consultant

Income

Begin with project *income*. Note the use of *grants, donations,* and *volunteer time*. Each is a possible source of community oral history project funding. (For definitions, see Appendix D of this volume and **Volume 1,** *Introduction to Community Oral History, Glossary.*)

Grants are funds awarded from community, city, state, and national organizations on a competitive basis. Writing and administering grants is time-consuming and requires specialized skills; project planners will want to base their budget recommendations on the availability of grant writers. They also will want to determine whether the available funds could be effectively used for a community oral history project and whether the time spent on grant writing would be an effective use of project resources and note this in a project plan.

Project income also can include *donations* solicited through fund-raising. Donations are funds usually given for specific project items. If a project may have access to people who can help raise funds for it, project planners may want to identify items on the proposed budget that can be targeted for donations. Even all-volunteer projects, like our fictitious *Project One—Volunteer,* can make use of donations for office supplies, photocopying, telephone, and other project support items.

Many project planners make use of *in-kind* support, especially if applying for grants. In-kind support means gifts or donations given in place of cash. It can include services of experts, offers of office and meeting space at no cost to the project, and use of recording equipment. The documented value of in-kind support also can be used with grant requests, since many applications ask for funding matches supplied through in-kind support as well as cash donations. During project planning, explore and document possible in-kind support options.

Volunteer help is another project budget category. Make recommendations on the use of volunteer and paid roles for project team members. Remember that volunteer help is a valuable contribution to a community oral history project and document it accordingly.

Projects applying for grant funding may need a *fiscal sponsor*—an organization not connected with the project that helps manage its finances. This is another consideration for project planners when defining possible income or funding sources, especially regarding the possible use of grants.

Expenses

Now let's look at possible project *expenses.* These include *one-time or non-recurring costs, overhead costs* and *per-interview costs.*

One-time or non-recurring costs are big-budget items. Recording equipment is the first item on the list of one-time expenses and can be the most expensive item in an oral history project budget. Equipment acquisition can be done through purchase or loan. Whatever decision is recommended, include equipment value in a proposed project budget.

Oral historians use external microphones. Microphones, along with a computer and good-quality cables for each recorder, are additional one-time costs. Budget one microphone for each recorder. Also plan to find or acquire a computer to dedicate to the project for office support, transcribing capability, and electronic interview storage. And, because oral history guidelines suggest you store multiple copies of project interviews in multiple places, add one or two external hard drives dedicated to electronic interview storage to the budget plan.

Transcribing equipment includes downloadable software designed for use with headphones and a foot pedal that can be purchased and plugged in to your computer's USB port. Add these costs to a proposed budget plan.

Depending on needs and resources, recommended big-budget items can be purchased, donated, or used on loan. Regardless of how you plan to acquire them, include a value for each as a line item in a project budget.

Overhead costs are project operating costs. These are items, such as paper, postage, photocopying and the like, that help keep a project running. When identified in a project proposed budget, directors can seek donations to cover the costs. If donated, the items can count as in-kind or matching costs for any grants the project may request. Include each item to document its projected value to a project.

Per-interview costs are the costs of doing an interview. They include pre-interview research expenses, costs of recording and preserving each interview, transportation figures, and other costs and fees incurred as part of the interview process. If you plan on developing a project archive, add archival supplies, processing, cataloging, and electronic storage (web hosting) costs to the list. Estimate these costs and document them in your proposed project budget, even if you expect some or all of the items to be donated.

"The Project has been sponsored by the Friends of the Greenwich Library since 1977, and submits its budget request to them annually.... The Project has a wonderful relationship with the Friends—the Chairman sits on the Friends Board—and the Library considers the Oral History Project to be a 'jewel' among its programs."

Greenwich (CT) Library Oral History Project, Catherine Ogden, Project Chair.

Taking each of our sample (fictitious) community oral history projects, let's examine possible budget planning needs.

- *Project One—Volunteer* The all-volunteer project may not pay its project team, but it still can benefit from donations and in-kind support; some all-volunteer projects may consider applying for grants to help defray some costs. If this is done, planners should recommend the project use a fiscal sponsor to manage grant funds.

- *Project Two—City* This project, done in conjunction with a city, makes use of grant funds but also, through its connection with the city, has access to in-kind support; project planners may opt to use a combination of paid and volunteer project team members with city financial personnel providing budget and grants management and city technical personnel providing equipment support.

- *Project Three—Historical Society* The ongoing program developed by the historical society probably will have access to similar support income and support options available to the city project. Planners will want to determine when and how to use these resources to give the program a strong start and organize spending to meet ongoing needs.

Funding Sources

The next step, after a project planning team has estimated project costs and proposed a budget, is to identify possible funding sources. Even all-volunteer projects have expenses and can use donations and in-kind support.

As you look for ideas for funds and support, identify core budget items—the things you cannot do without. Think first about support for these materials, and consider recommending the project approach supporters from within the community. Civic organizations, businesses and corporations, foundations, government sources, and individual supporters all are options. Most public libraries have grant and foundation materials in non-circulating, reference collections. Look for information about grant organizations or foundations with giving areas that match project goals, budget items, and application procedures. Grant-writing workshops also are helpful in learning more about giving options.

In addition to funding sources in the community, look for sources of support in your area and state. State historical societies, state humanities councils, state arts councils, and some agencies of state government often have grants opportunities. Attend the annual meetings of your state historical society, state humanities council, and state or regional oral history association. Review available grants guidelines to determine project eligibility. Many of these funding sources require a preliminary proposal for review before submission of a grant application, and most have specific requirements for amounts requested, budget items eligible for support, programming, project personnel, research methods, completion timelines, and project evaluation. All will have application deadlines, either a specific date or rolling dates throughout the year. Identify and recommend funding and support sources for the project and include information about each in the plan.

The following list shows examples of community oral history funding sources identified by the oral historians who responded to our questionnaire.

- self or private funding
- individuals
- businesses and corporations with ties to the community
- city, county, or state governments
- local, county or state historical societies, humanities councils, libraries, and museums
- ethnic, civic, and professional associations, clubs or interest groups, church organizations, labor organizations, and seniors organizations
- radio or television stations or newspapers
- schools, colleges, and universities
- private or public foundations, nonprofit organizations, or corporations
- national sources, including National Endowment for the Humanities

Use this list as a starting point for learning about what is available in your community. Look at support as a way of helping the project and strengthening the project's ties to the community.

"[We received] grants from The CA [California] Council for the Humanities, Southwest Oral History Assn., local donors and in-kind donations."

The Azusa (CA) Heritage Project, Luisa Miranda, Project Director

"The oral history program is supported by Chippewa Valley Museum's general operating resources (local government, memberships, earned income) as it is part of our core program. Since oral history is commonly one of the research strategies we use in major interpretive projects, it is frequently supported by grants and sometimes as the specific purpose of a particular grant, typically in advance of advanced development for a large project. For example, the Fields and Dreams Project was funded by the Wisconsin Humanities Council and the results used as an aspect of research for the major Farm Life project, later supported by the National Endowment for the Humanities."

Chippewa Valley Museum, WI, Susan McLeod, Director

Identifying and recommending support options for an oral history project plan takes time and research, but it can pay off. Community, state, and private options probably will offer the greatest chance for success. Funding from national sources, such as the National Endowment for the Humanities (NEH), is highly competitive; applicants must provide evidence of national significance and intensive planning.

When thinking about and reviewing possible community oral history project support, be aware that some supporters may have specific goals in mind. You also may run into rivalries among potential funders or supporters. Don't let this deter or sidetrack you. Recommend seeking support from all possible sources. Remember also to keep funding options for oral histories separate from project products. Although this may seem obvious, it can be tempting (or easier) to suggest funding sources for websites, exhibits, public programs, and documentaries rather than for doing the oral history interviews. Don't let oral history project needs get lost when searching for and identifying funding options.

Finally, remember that developing requests requires time and, in some cases, specific skills. Research the options so you know how to develop a successful approach. Some recommended sources may give your project a good return for time spent on a request, whereas others may be long shots or take more time than you can afford.

"[We received] grants from Clorox Foundation and SF [San Francisco] Foundation; some of OACC's [Oakland Asian Community Center] operating budget."

Oakland (CA) Chinatown Oral History Project, Angela Zusman, Project Manager

"We received university funding through the Center of Upper Peninsula Studies whose new task is to conduct oral interviews among other activities."

Marquette (MI) General Health Services Oral History Project, Russell M. Magnaghi, Project Director and Interviewer

Funding categories

With a mission statement in place and the project goals, focus, and scope defined, look into the types of funding available from the sources you have identified. Oral history project funding sources generally fall into several categories—*grants, donations,* and *solicited funds* (fund raised). Funding can be *cash, in-kind,* or *gifts of time.*

Projects receiving *grants* usually have to meet specific guidelines and show evidence of the ability to raise funds as a percentage match of the grant award. If you recommend applying for grants, determine whether you will manage an award through your project or will need a fiscal sponsor. Many grants agencies require that the project use a non-profit organization as a fiscal sponsor, especially for independent projects with no institutional ties. Depending on how your project will be organized, this can mean recommending the project recruit a partner to work in applying for funds from these sources.

If you can find a grant-writing workshop, sign up for it. Even if you have grant-writing experience, workshops are good sources of information about funds and fiscal sponsors. They also are good places to meet people to add to a proposed project supporters list.

Donations in the form of gifts and *solicited funds* help provide basic project support. *Cash* gifts always are helpful, as are *in-kind* donations. Include a list of potential supporters in the plan.

Volunteers, giving their time, are the backbone of many oral history projects. Define proposed volunteer team member roles and suggested values for these roles in a project plan.

CHAPTER 7

Winding Up

BEST PRACTICE NO. 3

Cast a wide net to include community.

BEST PRACTICE NO. 5

Make a plan.

BEST PRACTICE NO. 7

Train interviewers and other project participants
to assure consistent quality.

BEST PRACTICE NO. 9

Process and archive all interview materials to
preserve them for future use.

Several years ago, a group of Smith College alumnae active in the Smith Club of Minnesota approached the Minnesota Historical Society with a community oral history request. They had an idea about developing an alumnae oral history project and wanted advice on how to proceed. They formed the Smith Club of Minnesota oral history project planning committee and began developing a project. Guided by James E. Fogerty, Minnesota Historical Society oral historian, they developed the Smith College Club of Minnesota Oral History Project. They decided on a name, project director and team members, interviewees, interview topics, recording equipment, a project repository, a project product (a publication), and other project planning needs.

The club then sponsored two interviewer training workshops for volunteer alumnae club interviewers. Over a two-year period, volunteer interviewers completed sixteen fully-processed audio interviews. Using interview information, planning committee volunteers published a book about their interviewees.

After this phase, considered the pilot phase, the project director and team members developed Phase Two of the project. With new and returning interviewers, the alumnae club sponsored another interviewer training workshop and created a training DVD for use in future years. As with the pilot phase, Phase Two had a definite timeline for completion. It, too, resulted in fully processed interviews and a publication. Although each phase had a defined scope (duration and size), the project was designed so phases could be added on an ongoing basis. Given the large, and growing, potential interviewee pool, careful project planning allowed this all-volunteer group to set realistic goals and achieve them.

The planning steps in this chapter help finalize a plan for your community oral history project. Keep the information on the Project Design Statement in mind as you review each of these steps.

After-the-Interview Options

Once the interviews are complete, a project team undertakes a number of steps, generally called processing, that transform a raw interview into a finished oral history available to users now and in the future. These processing steps require planning in terms of people, office space, and computer equipment. **Volume 3,** *Managing a Community Oral History Project* discusses processing from a management perspective, and **Volume 5,** *After the Interview in Community Oral History* is devoted to processing from an archiving perspective. This chapter discusses processing from a planning perspective.

Processing actions fall roughly into the following categories, and all of them require planning. Review and discuss each one at this stage in preparing a community oral history project plan.

- record keeping
- media management
- transcribing
- repository
- Internet
- acknowledgements

"It [the interview] is not done until it is in a condition that can be used by researchers and the content reaches an audience."

Chippewa Valley Museum (WI), Susan McLeod, Director

"Catalogers have limited time and many items to work on. If they have to listen all the way through an oral history interview to determine how to catalog it, it probably won't get done as quickly as one that comes in with the cataloging information clearly identified and available."

Carla Johnson, Cataloging Services Librarian for the Southeast (MN) Library Cooperating/Southeast Library System (SELCO)[15]

Let's examine each category as part of the planning for after-the-interview.

Record keeping refers to identifying and filling in project forms and making sure these forms and all other project records are filed, organized, and accessible. See Chapter 4 of this volume for planning-related, record-keeping steps and **Volume 5,** *After the Interview in Community Oral History* for information about setting up a computerized record-keeping system.

As part of a record-keeping system, recommend using the Interview Summary form (see Chapter 4). This preliminary cataloging step provides immediate control over the interview. The more detail a summary contains, the more access it provides to interview information.

Media management covers media and interview recording storage decisions. For planning purposes, remember the standard oral history guideline: make multiple copies of each recording in multiple formats and store them in multiple places.

Next consider how to preserve the recordings. Will you store them on discs, will they be stored media free, or will you use both options? See **Volume 5,** *After the Interview in Community Oral History* for a detailed discussion about the options. Review and recommend options and include a statement about the importance of copying files to many locations and carefully labeling each copied file for storage purposes.

 Remember to be guided by LOCKSS (Lots of Copies Keeps Stuff Safe)

Transcribing Planning Guide	
Pros	*Cons*
Clarifies difficult-to-understand sections of the recording	Can be expensive and is time-consuming
Includes correct spelling of proper and place names	Cannot completely capture spoken or visual nuances in speech
Can be used as to develop an audio or video index	Can discourage listening or viewing of the interview recording
Almost always preferred by researchers	Is one more item to process, store, and catalog
Is user friendly; easy to browse and doesn't need special equipment	Some oral historians question its need in the digital age
Is the ultimate preservation format	
Is required by many repositories	

Table 7.1. Transcribing pros and cons.

Transcribing creates a word-for-word (verbatim) record of an interview. Transcribing requires time and commitment, but it preserves interview content in a form that can be easily accessed on an ongoing basis. Review the list of transcribing pros and cons provided in Table 7.1 to help you think through this planning decision.

Unless you have a firm commitment and ongoing support for unlimited, long-term data storage, refreshment, and migration, my coauthors and I strongly recommend you include a plan to transcribe your interviews. We also recommend project managers develop a transcribing guide that defines specific formats and guidelines for transcribers.[16]

A *repository* preserves oral histories and provides access to them. Repository personnel use cataloging records to describe items in a collection. Basically, cataloging means developing a systematic list of items in a collection. Information in catalog records comes from metadata—the sum total of information describing a resource, such as descriptive metadata (including interview summary information) entered by a cataloger; technical metadata about the digital file generated by the computer; or administrative metadata concerning location of resource, access, and use privileges, entered by an archivist. All metadata is packaged in a separate electronic envelope that travels with the digital resource throughout its life.

See Chapter 4 of this volume for a discussion of repositories. For planning purposes, recommend a repository and include a process to meet cataloging and metadata documentation needs from the beginning of project management.

"The best way to ensure that your oral history is preserved is to have it transcribed and printed out. If it is stored on a CD, only write in the hub. ... The future of archives will include 'trusted' digital repositories that will store data online. But this information will need to be continually migrated and is expensive. CDs are currently only guaranteed for about twenty years. If stored in a responsible archive, they could be re-created periodically to extend their life on CD. But, a paper transcript is still the most effective long-term (think 100-500 years) preservation methodology."

Rhonda Chadwick, MLS/Archives Degree Candidate, submission to the oral history listserv, June 19, 2010.

"We wanted the materials to be accessible for researchers and the transcript cannot really be beaten for accessibility. We also posted many on-line on the organization's website."

Worcester (MA) Women's History Project, Oral History Initiative, Lisa Krissoff Boehm, Project Consultant.

Using our sample (fictitious) oral history projects, here are examples of how cataloging might be covered in a community oral history project plan.

- *Project One—Volunteer* A small neighborhood oral history project, such as a church or local organization, may partner with a local historical society that has existing collecting guidelines for accepting oral histories and plan to follow their suggestions on preparing for preservation and access for the interviews.

- *Project Two—City* A grant-funded, one-time oral history project organized with a city might plan to partner with the public library to do all the processing (record keeping, transcribing, storage, access), and deposit the interviews in the library's special collections.

- *Project Three—Historical Society* A medium sized historical society with a physical site and volunteer staff might plan to develop a concept for an ongoing program, recruit volunteers to do the interviewing, do all processing in-house, keep all master files, provide user access on-site, and plan to partner with digital repository or larger library for broader access.

If you are working with a situation, as in two of our fictitious projects, where you will have assured access to a repository such as a city library or local historical organization, personnel there may take on some of the processing tasks. But even with a repository on board, project planners often have to include a certain amount of time for processing as a requirement for adding the project to a collection.

Processing actions regarding the *Internet* are discussed in Chapter 4 of this volume.

Acknowledgements include a reminder in the plan to thank your interviewees, recognizing their gift to your community. Give each one a copy of his or her transcript (and recording if they wish) and invite everyone to your final celebration.

Project Workshops and Training Materials

Careful and thorough interviewing by interviewers grounded in interview topics is critical to project success. Include a recommendation to develop project orientation and training materials that provide the following:

- project orientation material,
- an interviewer training manual, and
- a transcriber training manual.

Also include recommendations for the time and support needed to develop these materials. See **Volume 3,** *Managing Community Oral History Projects* for further details.

Training workshops

Oral history interviewers and transcribers, even experienced ones, benefit from training workshops. Training workshops provide an opportunity for them to review the resources and proposed project content and to become familiar with the project design. Interviewer training workshops generally last for a full day; to provide all participants with consistent information, planners should recommend mandatory attendance for all interviewers regardless of their background or previous experience. Transcriber training workshops generally are about a half-day long; planners should recommend mandatory attendance for all transcribers, unless the project will be using professional transcribing services or businesses.

Include interviewer and transcriber training workshops in your project plan. This supports our Best Practice No. 7: *Train interviewers and other*

"Thorough processing (transcript, abstract [summary], subject headings, cataloging) makes the [interview] content identifiable and accessible."

Cyns Nelson/Susan Becker, From Secrecy to Accessibility: The Rocky Flats (CO) Nuclear Weapons Plant Oral Histories

project participants to insure consistent quality. Include the development of project interviewer and transcriber training manuals as part of the workshop planning, and suggest basing these manuals on standard oral history manuals with adaptations made specifically for your project. See **Volume 3,** *Managing a Community Oral History Project,* for a detailed discussion of training manual content and workshop agendas.

Recap—Why Plan?

So how did we do in answering the Community Oral History FAQs about project planning from Chapter 1? Let's take a look. The nearby checklist provides a chapter reference for each of the FAQs.

COMMUNITY ORAL HISTORY FAQS

✓ *How long does it take to do an oral history project?*
   See **Chapter 3** for Project scope.

✓ *How many people from the community should we involve in our project?*
   The *Toolkit's* Best Practices for Community Oral History encourage planners to "cast a wide net." See **Chapter 2** for people planning steps, **Chapter 4** for project team options, and **Chapter 7** for sharing your plan in your community.

✓ *How about our community leaders? What is the best way to involve them?*
   See supporters discussion in **Chapter 2** and assembling a project plan in **Chapter 7.**

✓ *We want to do oral histories about our community, but everybody has a different idea about what this means. What should we do?*
   See **Chapter 3** for discussion of goals, focus, and mission statement.

✓ *How many people should we interview and who should they be?*
> See **Chapter 3** for goals, focus, scope, and mission statement and preliminary interviewee list.

✓ *How do we figure out what questions to ask during an interview?*
> See **Chapter 3** for Project Design Statement, goals, focus, scope, mission statement, interview content, and interview context.

✓ *Why do we need a Legal Release Agreement, especially if we're only doing a small project?*
> See **Chapter 1** for legal and ethical discussions.

✓ *What kind of equipment should we use? What about using our home video cameras to record our interviews?*
> See **Chapter 5** and **Appendix C** for review of equipment options.

✓ *Do we need a budget?*
> See **Chapter 6** for budget and funding discussion.

✓ *What should we do with the interviews after we've recorded them?*
> See **Chapter 7** for after-the-interview planning information.

✓ *We don't want our interviews to just sit on a shelf somewhere. How can we encourage people to use them?*
> See **Chapter 2** for legal and ethical discussion, **Chapter 4** for information about a repository and project forms and permissions, and **Chapter 7** for cataloging and additional after-the-interview planning information.

✓ *What do we have to do so we can use the interviews in our upcoming community celebration?*
> See **Chapter 2** for legal and ethical discussion, **Chapter 4** for information about a repository and project forms and permissions, and **Chapter 7** for after-the-interview planning information.

This is how oral history planning works; it takes the threads of discussion on many levels from the various planning steps and wraps them together to support oral history interviews. Use the information in this planning volume as a guide for your community oral history project; it will lay a strong groundwork for doing your interviews.

But don't stop here. Review all the *Toolkit* volumes; each includes a wealth of additional information to help answer basic questions about planning community oral history projects. And then, when you are ready, assemble a project plan and begin developing your oral history project.

Assemble Plan and Share it with Supporters

Now that you have covered all parts of the project plan, it is time to assemble it and share it with supporters. The plan should contain your decisions and recommendations for a community oral history project, and should include everything in the nearby checklist.

SUGGESTED PROJECT PLAN COMPONENTS

✓ Project Design Statement

✓ Names of the project planning team members and planning director

✓ Project name

✓ Project goals, focus, and scope

✓ Mission statement

✓ Preliminary list of interviewee names

✓ Oral history project member roles, including interviewers

✓ Names of community supporters

✓ Repository options

✓ Suggested forms, including Legal Release Agreement (donor form)

✓ Proposed budget and discussion of funding or support sources

✓ Equipment and media options

✓ After-the-interview options

✓ Training workshops

Share the project plan with the community. If you will be soliciting gifts or grants, use it as a tool in this process. The plan is your guide for recording your community's history.

 The project plan is your guide for recording your community's history.

The recommendation at the beginning of this volume to begin a community oral history project with a plan rather than with interviews may have surprised you. A project plan is a basic organizational tool that gets an oral history project off to a strong start. It provides a process for answering the

Community Oral History FAQs—the questions that commonly come up when doing community oral history and need to be dealt with. It also provides a structure for laying the solid groundwork we mention in our Best Practice No. 8: *Conduct interviews that will stand the test of time.* This is the heart of the oral history process, but its success depends on project design and structure. A plan also helps you develop the strongest interview support system available and, as such, lays the groundwork for the nuanced, in-depth interviews that will provide a valuable addition to the historical record.

Plan well, plan thoroughly, plan carefully. A solid oral history project plan is a gift to your community.

Planning Survey and Respondents

ORAL HISTORY PLANNING SURVEY
Community Oral History Toolkit

Please return by July 15, 2009

Several months ago, you participated in our first *Community Oral History Toolkit* survey. Thank you for agreeing to participate in this follow-up survey. It will be used to develop the community oral history toolkit, under contract with Left Coast Press, Inc. *Toolkit* authors are Nancy MacKay, Mary Kay Quinlan, and Barbara W. Sommer.

The focus of this survey is on the specifics of oral history project planning. Return to barbsom@aol.com by July 15, 2009. Questions? E-mail at the same address or call 651-797-3645. Thank you from Nancy MacKay, Mary Kay Quinlan, and Barb Sommer.

Project Name: _____

Project Topic: _____

Primary Goal: _____

- ❑ Collect oral histories
- ❑ Support exhibit development
  Exhibit title: _____
- ❑ Part of a festival or celebration
  Name of event: _____
- ❑ Community building
- ❑ Other—Describe: _____

Number of interviews:

_____ Scheduled

_____ Completed

Project Timeline:

Dates: _____

Repository:

Name: _____

Oral histories available through (check all that apply)

❏ library

❏ archive

❏ digital repository (Note: this does not include posting interviews online)

❏ other

    Describe: _____

1. Which of the following oral history planning steps did you do when developing your project and when did you do each step? Use a separate sheet to describe *Other* as needed.

Planning step	Before project	Beginning of project	During project	End of project	Other (describe)
Give project a name					
Write purpose/ mission statement					
Determine timeline					
Determine number of interviews					
Identify project personnel					
Identify narrator pool					
Identify interviewer(s)					
Make arrangements with repository					
Develop forms including legal release form					
Develop budget					
Decide on recording equipment					
Decide on recording media					
Determine processing techniques					
Develop interviewer training					
Develop publicity plan					

2. Identify team members by development and management responsibilities.

   Check all that apply. Use separate sheet to describe consultant duties as needed.

   If Project Director and Interviewer are the same person, check here_____.

Planning step	Project Director	Interviewer(s)	Clerical(s)	Budget officer	Consultant (describe)
Give project a name					
Write purpose/mission statement					
Determine timeline					
Determine number of interviews					
Identify project personnel					
Identify narrator pool					
Identify interviewer(s)					
Make arrangements with repository					
Develop forms including legal release form					
Develop budget					
Decide on recording equipment					
Decide on recording media					
Determine processing techniques					
Develop interviewer training					
Develop publicity plan					

3. Narrative Questions
   (use extra space as needed, bullet-point summaries are fine)

   - Describe your project.

- Describe overall planning process for your project.

- Which of the oral history planning steps did you find most helpful and why?

- Which of the oral history planning steps did you find least helpful and why?

- Describe project use of donor (legal release) form including where and how it was developed and copyright language used.

- Describe your equipment and media decisions.

- Describe your project budget including budget categories. Identify the most costly item in your budget and why. It is not necessary to include itemized budget figures, but it will be helpful to know your total budget range:

  ❏ less than $1,000   ❏ $1,000-$5,000   ❏ $5,001-$10,000

  ❏ $10,001-$25,000   ❏ $25,001-$100,000

  ❏ over $100,000 (amount if you wish to indicate _____)

- Describe your project funding sources.

- Describe choosing and working with a project repository.

- What processing techniques did you use and why?
  ❏ abstract   ❏ transcript   ❏ abstract and transcript

- Looking back, what would you say are one or two highlights of the project?

- Is there anything more you would like to tell us? Add your thoughts and comments.

4. Oral History Project Examples. Attach as many as you wish.
- ❏ Project Name
- ❏ Project Mission Statement
- ❏ Donor (Legal Release) Form
- ❏ Project Management Forms
- ❏ Project Budget indicating itemized categories
- ❏ Abstract
- ❏ Transcript Excerpt
- ❏ Agenda – Interviewer Training Session
- ❏ Publicity Plan
- ❏ Other (identify)

Survey Responder(s): _____

Organization/Position(s): _____

Address: _____

_____

_____

Telephone: _____

Email: _____

Website: _____

PLEASE RETURN BY JULY 15, 2009

THANK YOU VERY MUCH FROM ALL OF US. WE'LL KEEP YOU POSTED ON OUR RESEARCH

Nancy MacKay, Mills College and San Jose State University

Mary Kay Quinlan, University of Nebraska and Oral History Association Newsletter Editor

Barbara W. Sommer, independent scholar, St. Paul, MN

Yancie Zibowsky, project intern, San Jose State University, School of Library and Information Science

Thank you to our community oral history project planning survey respondents:

The Azusa Heritage Project, Azusa, CA. Luisa Miranda, Project Director, and Arthur Ramirez, Videographer/cameraman.

Bland County History Archives/Place-Based Education, Rocky Gap, VA. John Dodson, Director of the Bland County History Archives and the Mountain Home Center.

Chippewa Valley Museum, Eau Claire, WI. Susan McLeod, Director.

Dana Point Historical Society Oral History Project, Dana Point, CA. Mary A. Crowl, Director.

El Toro Marine Corps Air Station Oral History Project, Fullerton, CA. Janet Tanner, California State University, Fullerton, Center for Oral and Public History.

The Freight and Salvage: An Oral History, Berkeley, CA. Andrea Hirsig, Night Manager, Freight and Salvage Coffee House.

Greenwich Library Oral History Project, Greenwich, CT. Catherine H. (Cathy) Ogden, Chairman.

Iron Range Research Center, Chisholm, MN. Scott Kuzma, Director.

Leadership Interviews. Jewish Federation of Metropolitan Detroit, Bloomfield Hills, MI. Sharon Alterman, Director, Leonard N. Simons Jewish Community Archives, Jewish Federation of Metropolitan Detroit.

Mackinac Bridge Oral History Project, Lansing, MI. Michigan Oral History Association, Geneva Kebler Wiskemann, Founder/Secretary.

Marquette General Health Services, Marquette, MI. Russell M. Magnaghi, Project Director and Interviewer, Northern Michigan University, Director, Center for Upper Peninsula Studies.

Meaningful Stories, Meaningful Lives. JARC, Farmington Hills, MI. Karen Siersma Rosenstein, Judaic Services Coordinator.

Mexican Voices, Michigan Lives—Part II (I), East Lansing, MI. Diana Rivera, Chicano/Ethnic Studies Librarian, Michigan State University.

"Your Story and Mine: A Community of Hope," Lansing, MI. Martha Aladjem Bloomfield, Project Director, Michigan Historical Museum, Community Relations Liaison, and Michigan Humanities Consultant.

Oakland Chinatown Oral History Project, Oakland, CA. Angela Zusman, Project Manager, Phase 1.

"From Secrecy to Accessibility: The Rocky Flats Nuclear Weapons Plant Oral Histories," Boulder, CO. Susan Becker, Maria Rogers Oral History Program Manager; Cyns Nelson, Voice Preserve: Oral historian, archivist; LeRoy Moore, Rocky Mountain Peace and Justice Center; Hannah Nordhaus, oral historian, journalist.

Savannah Jewish Archives Oral Histories, Savannah, GA. Lynette Stoudt, Archivist, Savannah Jewish Archives (Senior Archivist, Georgia Historical Society), Kaye Kole, Project Director.

Smith College Club of Minnesota, Oral History Project, Eden Prairie, MN. Betsey Whitbeck, Smith College Club of Minnesota, President.

Surfing Heritage Foundation Oral History Committee, San Clemente, CA. Paul Holmes, Surfing Heritage Foundation Oral History Committee Chair.

Worcester Women's History Project, Oral History Initiative, Worcester, MA. Lisa Krissoff Boehm, Professor of Urban Studies, Project Consultant.

Equipment and Technology Terms

Technology can get technical. Use the list of definitions to stay on track in planning discussions about project equipment. See also **Volume 1, *Community Oral History,* Chapter 1** and **Glossary,** and the Glossary of Terms and Concepts on the Technology page, Oral History Association website (http://www.oralhistory.org/technology/digital-audio-recording-glossary-of-terms-and-concepts/).

bit Smallest unit of data on a computer with a single binary value of 0 or 1; a string of 8 bits is a byte.

> ***bit depth*** Potential accuracy of hardware or software; the larger the number of bits, the higher quality the recording.

> ***bit rate*** Number of bits processed in a given unit of time.

blu-ray Commercial term for an optical disc developed for use with high definition video.

broadcast quality Meets television production standards.

codec Algorithm in a computer program that reduces (compresses) the number of bytes in an electronic file for ease in storing and transmitting data.

> ***Lossless codec*** Saves data in a compressed format and reconstructs it as recorded.

> ***Lossy codec*** Saves data in a compressed format and reconstructs it as an approximation of the original recording.

compact disc (CD) Optical disc (disk) used for storage and access of sound and other types of data; CD sound quality is 16 bit/44kHz.

compress (reduce)/uncompress (unreduced) Remove bytes, reducing size of data file, according to a mathematical formula; uncompressed (unreduced) data in its original recorded form with no compression.

cross platform Operates with a variety of computer hardware designs and software programs.

data Information converted into binary (0s and 1s) system for digital recording, preservation, and access.

database A collection of related data that is organized so that its contents can easily be accessed, managed and updated.

digital A process that captures and stores sound by taking samples of sound waves, rather than the continuous signal.

digital versatile (video) disc (DVD) Optical disc (disk) used for storage and access of sound and video data.

file A unit of related data, often referred to as a document. A file can be a text document, a spreadsheet, an image or an audio file.

file extension A series of visible letters at the end of a file name added when a document is saved. Examples are .rtf (Rich Text. Format), .pdf (Portable Document Format), and .txt. (text).

format A term used to describe various categories and distinctions in information technology.

hardware Physical components of computers such as electronic circuitry.

high definition Picture and sound display technology.

Internet A global network that transmits digital electronic material.

management system A database system for keeping records for collections, projects, or online content.

master recording A recording that is preserved intact as recorded.

media Physical devices for capturing, storing, or preserving information.

memory card Solid state digital storage device.

metadata Data about data. Metadata about an interview includes all the information available about it.

microphones A device that converts sound to electrical signals, usually for amplification; though microphones occur inside recorders, external microphones provide higher quality sound and should be used for oral history interviews.

migration Process of transferring data files from one format to another.

open source Hardware and software publicly developed and freely available.

proprietary/non-proprietary Hardware and software owned exclusively and kept secret by one company; often designed to work only with the company products; non-proprietary refers to hardware and software publicly developed and freely available.

prosumer A consumer of electronic goods developed for professionals.

protocol Set of rules that guides transferring information on the World Wide Web; http is an example of a protocol.

recording unit A customized "package" for audio or video recording equipment; can include recorder, microphone, cables, and batteries.

sampling rate The number of samples from a sound wave that the computer takes to make a digital file; the larger the sample the higher the quality of sound and the more closely the digital sound represents the original.

solid state A popular new technology that uses data cards to record oral histories.

universal disc format File system standard that ensures consistency among data written to various optical media.

web hosting Digital storage on the World Wide Web, often with a cloud infra-structure; essential components include disc space (size allocation) and bandwidth (data transfer).

Recording Equipment Standards

This information for project technical advisers and technicians focuses on equipment that meets oral history recording standards.

Recorders

Look for high-quality, sturdy equipment that is available, portable, and easy to use.

Audio Recorder Features

Recording quality (measured in sample/sampling rate and bit depth)

- the current standard is 24bit/96 kHz; minimum standard is 16bit/44 kHz

File and format options

- can record in a widely available, non-proprietary, open-source, uncompressed, cross-platform format indicated by the file extensions .wav or .aiff

- has the option to save recordings as data files

Equipment features

- slot for removable, reusable memory card

- two external microphone jacks for mono or stereo recording with external microphone or ability to accommodate professional quality external microphone with XLR or most up-to-date connection

- display window that shows power level, the amount of recording time left on memory card, and sound level

- manual volume control

- headphone jack with ¼" TRS connector
- USB interface option to allow transfer of information to a computer
- metadata generator
- the basics—on/off switch, record, pause, and rewind switches
- AC adapter

For more, or updated, recording equipment information, see the Technology section of the Oral History Association website: http://www.oralhistory.org/technology. Your local library and local or state historical society also are good sources for updated information.

Video Recorder Features[17]

- Format: AVCHD (AVCCAM – Panasonic, NXCAM - Sony) or AVC-Intra-50 or AVC-Intra 100
- Compression: H.264/MPEG-4 AVC (set to highest possible recording quality in camera)
- Resolution: 1920x1080 60p, 30p or 60i or 1280x720 60p
- Frame Rate: 59.94i or 59.94p or 29.97p fps
- Aspect Ratio: 16:9 (All HD formats are native 16:9)
- Field Dominance: Upper Field First for 60i material, None for 60p or 30p
- Audio: PCM or AC3 at 24 bit/48 kHz (16 bit/48 kHz minimum) dB

Equipment features

- slot for removable, reusable memory card
- ability to accommodate professional quality microphones with XLR or most up-to-date connection
- can use a Y-cable or splitter when two microphones are needed on cameras with stereo mini microphone input
- display window/LCD screen
- manual volume control
- manual focus control
- zoom control
- manual white balance control
- manual exposure control

- display and data code button
- headphone jack with 1/8" mini headphone jack
- USB interface option to allow transfer of information to a computer
- ability to play back and review recordings
- the basics – on/off switch, record, pause, and rewind switches
- AC adapter

Check regularly with the Oral History Association, your local library, or your local or state historical society for updates on specifications and recording.

Microphones

Oral historians use external microphones to maximize sound quality. There are two types of microphones—condenser and dynamic. Both translate acoustical signals into electrical ones. Condenser microphones require use of a power supply (batteries). They are sensitive to sound and often are used in music studios. Dynamic microphones generate their own current, eliminating the need for a power supply. They are sturdy and rugged and work well for voice recordings.

Microphones have two channels—mono and stereo.

- Mono microphones record one channel of sound
- Stereo microphones record two channels, left and right
- They have several pick-up patterns:
  - Omnidirectional microphones pick up all sound in a circular field around the microphone
  - Bidirectional microphones pick up sounds in a figure eight pattern in front of and behind the microphone
  - Cardioids, or directional, microphones pick up sound in a heart-shaped pattern from the microphone outward

I recommend:

- one dynamic, mono or stereo, omnidirectional, single-stand microphone that can pick up all voices in the interview, or
- directional lavaliere microphones—for each interview participant

Single stand microphones often are used for audio interviews. Oral historians use lavalieres both for audio and video interviews.

Accessories

Audio and video recording equipment accessories

Look for accessories that fit the needs of your project.

Media

Oral historians usually work with recorders that use removable, reusable solid state data-storage devices such as memory cards, such as CompactFlash (CF), Secure Digital (SD), and Secure Digital High Definition (SCHD) cards. When choosing media:

- Use removable cards if possible.

- Make sure media storage space is large enough to meet interviewing needs. For example, look for cards that allow for at least six hours of recording time at 24 bit/96 kHz.

Other

Oral historians use a variety of additional accessories. I recommend:

- headphones to monitor sound level and recording quality
- cables
  - cables and connectors that are shielded to reduce interference
  - cables and cords that are long enough to allow for maximum flexibility in positioning the recorder
  - recommended inputs - XLR or 1/4" TRS (Tip-Ring Sleeve) or most up-to-date - for a balanced, mono signal; two inputs for stereo recording
- USB card reader or cable to transfer recording from memory card to computer hard drive.

Video Equipment Accessories

In addition to standard recording equipment accessories, you will want the following for video interviews:

- tripod to balance the camera; recommend one with a fluid head and a leveling bubble
- lights—generally soft light or lights with diffusion gel
- reflectors—handheld or mounted with disc options for silver, gold, white, and black
- video monitor—provides a larger view of the image; use to review

framing, lighting, exposure and focus. Make sure the monitor can accept the type of signal the camera outputs; for HD this is usually component (red, green, and blue connectors) or HDMI.

Check carefully to determine which video accessories you may need. Use accessories that are compatible with your recorder.

Storage space

Storage Space Requirement Example: Audio
Sample needs for 60 minutes of audio recorded in unreduced 16bit/44.1 kHz:

- 600-800 megabytes

Sample needs for 60 minutes of audio recorded in unreduced 24bit/96 kHz:

- 2 gigabytes

Storage Space Requirement Examples: Video
Sample/sampling data rates for 60 minutes of video recorded at 1920x1080 30p or 60i:

- AVCHD - 11.8 gigabytes
- AVC-Intra 50 - 23.5 gigabytes
- AVC-Intra 100 - 46.0 gigabytes
- Uncompressed 10 Bit YUV - 597.6 gigabytes (no camera actually does this; figure included for comparison)

Computers

Computer features that are useful for oral history projects include:

- the highest speed processor and largest amount of RAM (Random Access Memory) the budget allows (speed)
- as much hard drive and access to external hard drives as the budget allows (storage)
- media player and audio and/or video editing software
- optimized processor for image manipulation
- USB 3, USB 2, FireWire, eSATA, Fiber Optic, and Thunderbolt or other current high speed data connections
- built-in redundancy

External Hard Drives

- Use 1 to 2 external hard drives for back-up storage.
- Choose external hard drives that include options for automatically monitoring data file integrity.

Budget and Funding Terms

Terms referred to in Chapter 6 are specific to budget and fiscal needs and to policies. The definitions here are a guide to their use in the planning process. See also **Volume 1,** *Community Oral History,* **Chapter 1** and **Glossary.**

challenge grant A grant with a defined challenge amount that must be met before funds are distributed.

cost-share Division of project costs for support by project and another source or sources.

fiscal sponsor An organization that takes responsibility for the finances of an unrelated party.

foundation A non-profit, charitable organization.

grant Funds given for a defined purpose.

in-kind Support given in goods or services rather than cash.

matching funds Funds or in-kind goods or services supplied by a grant applicant in an amount that matches grant funds.

nonprofit (also called not-for-profit) An organization that distributes funds for specifically defined goals rather than to shareholders.

re-grant Disperse funds received from another source.

self-funded When an individual or organization pays the full project cost without funding from outside sources.

subsidy Financial assistance from a governmental unit or other source.

volunteer Work given without payment.

NOTES

1. Mary Kay Quinlan and Barbara W. Sommer, *The People Who Made It Work: A Centennial Oral History of the Cushman Motor Works* (Lincoln, NE: Textron, Inc., 2001):105-106.

2. The Minnesota Commission for Deaf, DeafBlind, and Hard of Hearing Minnesotans Oral-Visual History Project, Minnesota Commission for Deaf, DeafBlind, and Hard of Hearing Minnesotans, http://www.mncdhh.org/ news/480/watch-the-oral-visual-history-stories-of-deaf-deafblind-and-hard-of-hearing-minnesotans, accessed April 17, 2012.

3. See also Laurie Mercier and Madeline Buckendorf, *Using Oral History in Community History Projects,* the Oral History Association, 2007:1,2,4.

4. Oral History Association, www.oralhistory.org, accessed March 24, 2012.

5. James A. Ballentine. *Ballentine's Law Dictionary, 3rd Edition (*Rochester, NY: The Lawyer's Co-Operative Publishing Co., 1969):272.

6. For more information, see: John A. Neuenschwander, *A Guide to Oral History and the* Law (New York, Oxford University Press, 2009) and *Oral History and the Law,* 3rd, ed., John Neuenschwander for the Oral History Association, 2002.

7. John Neuenschwander, *A Guide to Oral History and the Law* (New York: Oxford University Press, 2009):64.

8. See *A Guide to Oral History and the Law,* pp. 64-72, 79, for a full discussion of these topics. Although copyright does not need to be filed for copyright protection of oral histories, it must be registered before an infringement lawsuit can be filed.

9. John Neuenschwander, *A Guide to Oral History and the Law* (New York: Oxford University Press, 2009):5. See Volume One – An Introduction to *Community Oral History,* for a full set of sample *Toolkit* forms.

10. Barbara W. Sommer and Mary Kay Quinlan, *The Oral History Manual,* 2nd ed. (Walnut Creek, CA: AltaMira Press, 2009):23.

11. Laurie Mercier and Madeline Buckendorf, *Using Oral History in Community History Projects* (Oral History Association: 2007):10.

12. Barbara W. Sommer and Mary Kay Quinlan, *The Oral History Manual,* 2nd ed. (Walnut Creek, CA: AltaMira Press, 2009):11.

13. See also: Oral History Association, Technology page, http://www.oralhistory. org/technology/. Baylor Institute for Oral History, Digital Oral History Workshop, Digital Video Recording, http://www.baylor.edu/content/services/ document.php/79770.pdf.

14. Jesse Heinzen, email message to Barbara W. Sommer, June 6, 2012.

15. Carla Johnson, telephone conversation with Barbara W. Sommer, August 24, 2010.

16. As of this writing, equipment that transcribes directly from voice to text is not yet fully developed for oral history use. See Further Reading in this volume for transcribing guide citations.

17. Minnesota Historical Society, "Collection Management System: Video Formats," prepared by Jesse Heinzen, email to Barbara W. Sommer, January 3, 2012.

Books

MacKay, Nancy. *Curating Oral Histories: From Interview to Archive.* Walnut Creek, CA: Left Coast Press, Inc., 2007.

Neuenschwander, John A. *A Guide to Oral History and the Law.* New York, Oxford University Press, 2009.

Ritchie, Donald A. *Doing Oral History: A Practical Guide,* 2nd ed. New York: Oxford University Press, 2003.

Sommer, Barbara W. and Mary Kay Quinlan. *The Oral History Manual,* 2nd ed. Lanham, MD: AltaMira Press, 2009.

Trimble, Charles E., Barbara W. Sommer, and Mary Kay Quinlan. *The American Indian Oral History Manual: Making Many Voices Heard.* Walnut Creek, CA: Left Coast Press, Inc., 2008.

Pamphlets

Mercier, Laurie, and Madeline Buckendorf, *Using Oral History in Community History Projects,* for the Oral History Association, 2007.

Neuenschwander, John A. *Oral History and the Law,* 3rd ed., for the Oral History Association, 2002.

Articles

Boyd, Doug. "Preserving the Past," presentation at Oral History Preservation 101 Workshop, Kentucky Oral History Commission, Kentucky Historical Society, June 3, 2008.

Henson, Pamela. "From Analog to Digital: The Smithsonian Institution Archives Digital Preservation Initiative" in *The Oral History Association Newsletter,* Winter 2009:XLIII:3.

Preserving State Government Digital Information: Digital Audio and Video White Paper, unpublished paper, Minnesota Historical Society, May 2009.

"Boyd describes efforts to develop best digital practices for oral history" in *The Oral History Association Newsletter,* Winter 2011:XLV:3.

Websites

Capturing the Living Past: An Oral History Primer. An oral history tutorial on the Nebraska State Historical Society, http://www.nebraskahistory.org/lib-arch/research/audiovis/oral_history/index.htm, accessed January 26, 2012.

Federal Agencies Digitization Guidelines Initiative Audio Visual Working Group, http://www.digitizationguidelines.gov/audio-visual, accessed November 29, 2010.

Library of Congress Packard Campus for Audio-Visual Conservation, http://www.loc.gov/avconservation/packard/, accessed June 7, 2012.

"Making Sense of Oral History," *History Matters: The U.S. Survey Course on the Web,* http://historymatters.gmu.edu/mse/oral, accessed December 13, 2011.

Minnesota Historical Society Oral History Collection, The Minnesota Historical Society, http://www.mnhs.org/collections/oralhistory/oralhistory.htm, accessed February 28, 2012.

Oral History, Digital Oral History Workshop, Digital Video Recording, Baylor Institute for Oral History, http://www.baylor.edu/oralhistory/index.php?id=61236, accessed August 8,1 2012.

Oral History in the Digital Age (OHDA) guidelines. http://ohda.matrix.msu.edu, accessed September 15, 2012.

Oral History in the Digital Age (OHDA), Oral History Association (OHA). http://www.oralhistory.org/resources/oral-history-in-the-digital-age/, accessed September 15, 2012.

Oral History in the Digital Age: Making Sense of Oral History, http://ohda.matrix.msu.edu/2012/08/making-sense-of-oral-history/, accessed August 9, 2012.

Oral History/Oral History Workshop for Teachers (Parts I-IV and Quiz), Baylor Institute for Oral History, http://www.baylor.edu/oral_history/index.php?id=56907, accessed June 10, 2010.

Oral History/Oral History Workshop for Students (Parts 1-4 and Quiz), Baylor Institute for Oral History, http://www.baylor.edu/oral_history/index.php?id=56194, accessed June 12, 2010.

"Style Guide for Transcribing Oral History," Institute for Oral History at Baylor University, http://www3.baylor.edu/Oral_History/Styleguiderev.htm, accessed November 19, 2007.

Transcribing, Editing, and Processing Guidelines" of the Minnesota Historical Society, http://www.mnhs.org/collections/oralhistory/ohtranscribing.pdf, accessed November 19, 2007.

Organizations

Oral History Association, an organization of oral history practitioners, www.oral-history.org, accessed August 8, 2012.

The Consortium of Oral History Educators, http://www.umbc.edu/mrc/cohe/index.html, accessed August 8, 2012. Oral History Listserv, H-Local, an international network for scholars and professionals active in studies related to oral history, http://www.h-net.msu.edu/~oralhist

INDEX

Barbara W. Sommer, M.A., has more than thirty-five years' experience in the oral history field. She has been principal investigator and director of more than twenty major oral history projects and has taught at the University of Nebraska-Lincoln, Nebraska Wesleyan University, and Vermilion Community College, MN. She is author of many key publications in the field, including, with Mary Kay Quinlan, *The Oral History Manual*, 2nd ed. (AltaMira Press, 2009) and with Quinlan and Charles E. Trimble, *The American Indian Oral History Manual: Making Many Voices Heard* (Left Coast Press, Inc., 2008). Her award-winning book *Hard Work and a Good Deal: The Civilian Conservation Corps in Minnesota* (Minnesota Historical Society Press, 2008) draws on oral history interviews about the Civilian Conservation Corps.

Nancy MacKay, MLIS, has been straddling the line between libraries and oral history for more than twenty years. As a librarian she has worked with special collections, cataloging, and music in various academic settings. As an oral historian she teaches, consults, advises, and writes about oral history, especially oral history and archives. She directed the oral history program at Mills College, from 2001-2011, and currently teaches library science and oral history at San Jose State University. Nancy is the author of *Curating Oral Histories* (Left Coast Press, Inc., 2007).

Mary Kay Quinlan, Ph.D., is an associate professor at the University of Nebraska-Lincoln in the College of Journalism and Mass Communications. She has held positions at the University of Maryland, and has served as president of the National Press Club. She is editor of the Oral History Association Newsletter and co-author with Barbara Sommer of *The Oral History Manual*, 2nd ed. (AltaMira Press, 2009), *Native American Veterans Oral History Manual* (Nebraska Foundation for the Preservation of Oral History, 2005), and *Discovering Your Connections to History* (AASLH, 2000). She is also a co-author with Sommer and Charles E. Trimble of *The American Indian Oral History Manual: Making Many Voices Heard* (Left Coast Press, Inc., 2008).

green press
INITIATIVE

Left Coast Press, Inc. is committed to preserving ancient forests and natural resources. We elected to print this title on 30% post consumer recycled paper, processed chlorine free. As a result, for this printing, we have saved:

2 Trees (40' tall and 6-8" diameter)
1 Million BTUs of Total Energy
145 Pounds of Greenhouse Gases
786 Gallons of Wastewater
53 Pounds of Solid Waste

Left Coast Press, Inc. made this paper choice because our printer, Thomson-Shore, Inc., is a member of Green Press Initiative, a nonprofit program dedicated to supporting authors, publishers, and suppliers in their efforts to reduce their use of fiber obtained from endangered forests.

For more information, visit www.greenpressinitiative.org

Environmental impact estimates were made using the Environmental Defense Paper Calculator. For more information visit: www.papercalculator.org.